THE

EST? 1742

WHITBREAD
BOOK OF
SCOUSEOLOGY®

by
PHIL YOUNG and JIM BELLEW

VOLUME THREE—
MERSEYSIDE AT PLAY

THE WHITBREAD BOOK OF SCOUSEOLOGY VOLUME THREE — MERSEYSIDE AT PLAY

ISBN 0 9512781 2 6

Published by Scouse Promotions Ltd.
8 Mathew Street, Liverpool L2 6RE
Telephone: 051-236 1729

Printed by C.G.S. Print Group,
Poole Hall Industrial Estate,
Ellesmere Port, South Wirral L66 1ST

Cover Design — George Baxendale

Scouse Promotions Ltd. are members of the
Merseyside Tourism Board

The publishers wish to thank:
**Peter Hobbs and Tony Garforth of Whitbread for their
sponsorship and commitment to Scouseology.**

The Liverpool Echo for their kind co-operation and
access to their magnificent picture library.

Scouseology is a registered trade mark.

THE SCOUSEOLOGY COLLECTION

Whitbread Book of Scouseology — A-Z anthology of
People, Places and Events.

Volume 2 — Merseyside Life 1900-1987
Volume 3 — Merseyside at Play

Scouseology — The Calendar 1989
Scouse Passports — The Fun Never Sets on Merseyside

THE AUTHORS' FOREWORD
Welcome to Beatleland

As I turned into Mathew Street, the Jolly Gent wearing the colourful bandsman's uniform gave his long white moustache a twirl. "We hope you will enjoy the show" he said. He couldn't be the Sergeant could he? As I mingled with the multi national faces and languages I could hear the music. All those familiar lines, that gorgeous trumpet from Penny Lane, the stunning harmonies of Eleanor Rigby, the fun beat of Yellow Submarine. The Street was somehow familiar but different.

There was a glass roof over me and the colours and sounds made it seem as though I was stepping on to an L.P. Sleeve. *That* L.P. Sleeve. Cavern Walks was still there but the music spilled out of the Club onto the Street "I'm fixing a hole where the rain gets in . . ." The shops were a little different too. One was displaying collarless jackets, grey ones, for sale, together with their other goods. The coffee shop was like stepping back in time to 1963. So this is what it must have been like. A Japanese girl was placing a garland of flowers around the neck of John's statue, as an American took her photo. A meter maid called Rita was having her photo taken with some German boys. A horse called Henry was dancing a Waltz. Not a real horse of course, but he *could* dance. A Mr. Kite was setting up a trampoline and rings. Direct from Bishopgate the sign said, and everywhere the music and the colour.

I went back into the Street, passed the Wine Bar with people sitting outside under pretty umbrellas, passed the memorabilia shop and the restaurants. (Good, the Armadillo and the Casa Italia were still there). A guide dressed in a similar bandsman's uniform as the one I'd seen the 'Sergeant' wearing was giving directions and everywhere the music and the colour. And people spending money. It was Sunday in Beatleland but it could have been a Monday or a Thursday I suppose.

But it was a dream. I woke up. It was a dream wasn't it? Yes, but one of those dreams that could come true. Couldn't it?

Lennon made his controversial comments about the Beatles' popularity in 1966. What has little or no controversy is that the Beatles are more popular than Shakespeare — and look at Stratford-upon-Avon.

As it is, thousands of people come to Liverpool every year in search of the Beatles. The Merseyside Tourism Board run daily tours to Beatles sights and old haunts. Cavern City Tours arrange a variety of short or long stays and are responsible for the annual August Beatles Convention — and the people come from all over the world. Not just the people of that era trying to recapture some of the spirit of their youth and to indulge in a little nostalgia. Oh no, not just those babies.

What about the guy in his mid 20's who approached Liverpool for the first time on the ferry from Woodside. The day was wet and dark, and the continuous rain was almost obliterating the famed Pierhead skyline. Nevertheless, our American visitor was clicking away with an overworked camera and as the ferry was about to berth he accompanied his final shot by turning to one of the tour guides excitedly 'This sure beats the hell out of Florida'.

Or the two Italians having completed the same journey who scrambled off the ferry and went down on their knees, Pope style, to kiss the ground.

Inevitably there are amusing stories of Beatle visitors. Such as the one who having attended a Town Hall reception soon after his arrival turned to one of his hosts saying "Well it's really wonderful but I do need to freshen up, can you tell me which room I'm in?" Liverpool Town Hall taken over by Trust House Forte! Or the visitor who lost his camera which happened to be found by that doyen of Liverpool DJs, Bob Wooler. The organisers, aware that such a distinguished Beatle person as Bob finding the camera would be a thrill for the visitor to remember, arranged the meeting.

'Tom' they said 'do you know who this is?'

'Yes' said Tom 'it's the man who found my camera.'

So they come. Young and old from all corners of the world to look at Strawberry Fields, to try to get a glimpse of the banker or the fireman at Penny Lane, to visit the Casbah and Menlove Avenue, Joseph Williams School, the Inny (sorry it's gone) Quarry Bank (sorry it's changed its name) and all the other Beatle related locations, significant or not. They come on a pilgrimage to the City that spawned the century's most famous music makers. To see the sights, soak up the atmosphere and spend money. How should we greet them? How can we make sure they're not disappointed? And how can we make sure they will come back again and again. It wasn't a dream . . . was it?

Tête-à-Tête at the Walker.

MERSEYSIDE AT PLAY

ART FOR ART'S SAKE
or 'Who drank my Exhibit?'

In 1957 John Moores, head of the Littlewoods empire, decided to sponsor an exhibition-cum-competition at Liverpool's Walker Art Gallery. Moores, then 61 years old, had taken up painting as a serious hobby five years earlier, but by this time it had become his main leisure interest. "Painting is the ideal relaxation for the middle-aged man" he said. "Business is my first love — it always has been — but painting is my second. It has even taken priority over golf."

Since that first exhibition in November 1957, the biennial show has become one of the best known events on the European Art calendar. As with much of modern art, controversy has never been far from the surface. In 1978 many an eyebrow was raised at the £3,000 second prize winner, "Untitled No. 9". To you or I it just looked like a white canvas in a frame, but to the artist, William Turnbull it was, "basically a study of various shades of white worked over a blue ground with a palette knife.

"I think my pictures are very full. Some pictures are full of reds and yellows and blues, but this shows variations of white and the modulations are closer. There are ten or fifteen layers of paint with many colours mixed in."

In 1985 the exhibition catalogue printed a photograph of one of the entries on its side instead of upright, understandable really because to the layman it looked like a stain on a carpet. Unfortunately the artist, Ian Stephenson, principal lecturer in painting at the Chelsea School of Art, who had spent ten years painstaking work developing the painting was less than pleased: "It has a top and a bottom. It does matter to me."

One of the best known works to win the exhibition was David Hockney's "Peter getting out of Nick's pool." In 1978, eleven years after winning, the painting was at the centre of a row in John Moores' own headquarters, the JM Centre. Prudish office girls objected to Peter's naked backside adorning their corridor walls and so one of the most notable works of figurative art was sent to a storeroom at the Walker Art Gallery. The thoughts of 'Mr. John', who had arranged for the picture, along with many others, to be exhibited in the offices are not known.

One of the best features of the exhibition has been the debate it has stimulated. Support and criticism has sometimes come from unexpected quarters; witness Arthur Dooley writing about the 1965 exhibition. "It is representative of a certain bad trend in some of the London galleries, and in the art schools, which are under their influence. The exhibits concentrate on colour and form — there is absolutely no content, no trace of the individual. You cannot criticise this sort or art because there are no standards upon which it bases itself. It doesn't say anything. It doesn't move anyone. It is no more art than a new suit . . . This exhibition is a joke among Liverpudlians, because it almost automatically excludes anything that might be genuine art — Michaelangelo wouldn't have stood an earthly with the selection committee of this exhibition . . . Perhaps the worst feature of exhibitions like this, is that they put people off art."

Strong words, Arthur, but for all the criticisms, and laughs, directed at the exhibition, it has, since 1957, ensured that once every two years Merseyside is at the centre of the art world and, indeed, may have helped influence the siting of the Tate at Albert Dock.

William Turnbull with "Untitled No. 9".

David Hockney with 'Peter getting out of Nick's pool'.

"What do you think Al? Should I put it in the John Moores?" — *"Well Arthur, it looks just like the inside of my old Philips radiogram after it caught fire, it must be in with a shout."*
(Owen and Dooley with Arthur's Vietnam Pieta.)

AND OF COURSE HENRY THE HORSE . . . . . .

In the mid 19th century a Danish travelling showman, Charles Milton Hengler arrived in Liverpool, and, shrewd judge that he was, decided that since he was in the entertainment business, this was the place to be.

He opened a circus in Dale Street in 1855, but the landlord sold the site and he was forced to close down in 1861. He opened another in Newington, in the same year, but that was later demolished.

He moved on, but once he had acquired sufficient capital, he returned to Liverpool and bought a site in West Derby Road to build a "handsome and commodious hippodrome."

Hengler's Grand Cirque, or as it was universally known Hengler's Circus opened on Monday, November 13th, 1876, with a circus spectacular starring the Jackley Troupe. For a quarter of a century Hengler's was renowned for bringing the very best in international entertainers to the city; perhaps even the Hendersons and Mr. Kite. Always popular were the children's Christmas shows, the first of which was the quaintly named "The Fairy's Garden Party in Honour of Little Red Riding Hood."

Following the closure of the Circus in 1901 the building re-opened on August Bank Holiday 1902 as the Royal Hippodrome Theatre of Varieties, at the time the most up-to-date theatre in the country; the 'Hippy' was born. For thirty years the bills at the 'Hippy' read like a who's who of Music Hall, Houdini, Little Tich, the Two Bobs — probably the first duet singers of syncopated songs, Charlie

Henglers.

Hippodrome programme 1902.

Chaplin, Rob Wilton, George Robey, George Formby Snr., The Great Hackenschmidt, and Fred Karno. Once, in the days before the First World War, the stage, the largest in Liverpool, accommodated a boxing ring for a demonstration by the World Heavyweight Champion, Jack Johnson.

For thirty years music hall was king, but in 1931 the theatre was given over to the 'talkies'.

The last night of vaudeville, June 20th, 1931 was one of the city's most boisterous theatrical nights ever. The packed house greeted every act with almost fanatical enthusiasm, Fred Barnes, Fred Russell and Zeta Mor could hardly be heard and Harry Champion's rendition of "Any Old Iron" nearly brought the house down. The interval community singing overran and the show closed with Vesta Victoria performing "The Old Tin Kettle", "Now I Have to call him Father," and finally "Waiting at the Church" leaving an emotional audience cheering for more.

Just one month later the 'Hippy' reopened as a cinema, the first presentation being "Dracula" with Bela Lugosi which played to an audience of over 30,000 in one single week. Ironically Hengler's Circus had been one of the first places in the city to show moving pictures when in 1897 an audience who were watching "Dyson's Diorama and Gypsy Choir," were astonished to see pictures of waves actually breaking over a rocky beach, followed by a showing of the Lumiere Brothers pioneering classic, of a train coming into a station.

But just like circus and music hall before them, the movies had their day, and in May 1970, the 'Hippy' closed its doors for the last time as a place of entertainment; the last film shown was Paul Newman in "Winning".

Perhaps as we travel down West Derby Road we should sometimes pause and give a little thought to the sawdust ring, the laughter of the Saturday night music hall crowd, and the flickering romance of the back row at the movies that made the 'Hippy' unique.

The 'Hippy' in 1941.

The last film at the 'Hippy'.

THE MOLE OF EDGE HILL

There's nothing wrong with a bit of digging on a Sunday afternoon. The gardens of Merseyside bloom under the tender loving care of thousands of silently complaining husbands who, for the sake of a quiet life, toil away in the sun, praying for rain with all the fervour of an England cricket captain facing the West Indies . . . sorry a bevvy of England cricket captains facing the West Indies.

For one man digging became more than a spare time activity, it became an obsession. Joseph Williamson came from Warrington to Liverpool in 1780. He was a poor man but soon found a job in the Wolstenholme Square factory of a tobacco merchant called Thomas Moss Tate. He worked hard and impressed his boss so much that in 1802 he did the sensible thing and married the boss's daughter, Elizabeth. His wedding day behaviour was bizarre to say the least, he turned up at the church, St. Thomas's, Park Lane, in the full hunting regalia, and immediately after the ceremony he told his bride to go home and get his dinner ready. He, meanwhile, leapt on his horse and galloped off to meet the Liverpool Hunt.

He became well-known as an eccentric but from 1818 his eccentricity was channelled into one extraordinary avenue, he began to burrow. By now a wealthy man, Williamson had a large house, land and property in the area of Mason Street, Edge Hill. His Mason Street house was built on a foundation of sandstone, and, starting from his own cellar, he began to excavate a series of subterranean passages and huge underground halls, which was to become his own underground kingdom.

He didn't do all the work himself, and there was more than a hint of charity in his employment of out of work labourers. Once, he was sitting on a Poor Aid Committee he lost his temper with the smug worthies around him. "Do any of you employ labourers?" he shouted, then, he ushered them to a nearby yard and pointed to 50 or so men beavering away at seemingly meaningless tasks — carting heaps of stones from one place to another, or pumping water into and out of a well. Aimless maybe, but they were all receiving a weekly wage from Williamson, enjoying the benefits of charity without the loss of self-respect. Was he a forerunner of the Manpower Services Commission?

As the years went by, so his kingdom grew. Mile after mile of tunnels snaked their tortuous paths beneath Edge Hill. The only access to his underworld was via a heavy wooden door in his cellar, and visitors were not encouraged. He died in 1840 and was buried in the Tate family vault in St. Thomas's Churchyard. The church was demolished in 1905 and all the graves removed, except, for reasons lost in the mists of time, Williamson's. Unmarked, it lies there till this day, on that triangle of land at the junction of Paradise Street and Park Lane.

His grave may be there but I fancy Williamson isn't in it. Late at night returning from London on the Euston train, as the light switches from the orange and black of the city night, to the many shades of black of the Edge Hill tunnels, on the approach to Lime Street, you can sometimes see figures in the recesses and side tunnels. Could this be Williamson's army? You blink and they're gone.

Around you, people reach for suitcases and coats, mouldering students, railcards in hand, yawn and stretch like shaggy brown bears coming out of hibernation, semi-comatose tattooed young men, with shaved heads stir, disturbing mounds of rejected beer cans, and ladies from Woolton and Formby with sunbed tans, beige leather trousers, and Access cards, cuddle their Harrods' shopping bags.

You press your face to the window, straining your eyes. And there he is. A great shambling bear of a man, his hat a battered topper of once-fine beaver skin, his coat, patched and snuff coloured, his corduroy trousers stained with the red sandstone earth, his hobnailed boots filthy. Could it be? . . . Could it be? . . .

No it's just another British Rail employee.

The Mole.

THE WILD ROVER

This Salford born footballer holds the rare distinction of having played for Everton, Liverpool and Tranmere Rovers, but never played in a league 'derby' game. His list of clubs reads like a British Rail timetable: Everton, Aston Villa, Huddersfield Town, Everton again, Liverpool, Cambridge City, Bury, Tranmere Rovers, Ballymena, Ellesmere Port Town, Fleetwood, Ballymena again, and finally Bangor (Northern Ireland). He is, of course, the incomparable Dave Hickson.

Raised in Ellesmere Port he signed professional for the Blues in May 1948, after joining the club as a 15-year-old. He made his league debut against Leeds United at Elland Road on September 1, 1951, and soon made his mark, in more ways than one, on opposing defenders and referees' notebooks. He was, never less than totally committed and his all action style quickly earned him the nickname of 'Dirty Dave' from opposing fans. He asked for no quarter from his opponents and during his career was on the receiving end of a fair number of 'X' certificate tackles. His courage was never in doubt and on more than one occasion he battled through a match with blood pouring from a head wound. Referees, however, took a different view of Dave's playing style and during his career he was suspended three times, but on many occasions he had talked his way into the book. At one time he was undoubtedly a marked man by the game's officials. The story is told that once, sitting on a train at Lime Street Station, he heard a guard's whistle blow and popped his head out of the window, asking "What have I done now, ref?".

Dave never achieved any of the great honours in the game, his most lasting impression on the record books is probably scoring the goal against Birmingham City that clinched promotion for the Blues in 1954. Unfortunately, as Everton were going up, Liverpool were going down and Dave missed those 'derby' opportunities.

It is hard to imagine now the furore when Hickson 'crossed the Park' in November 1959 for the princely sum of £10,500. The local press was full of letters from fans of both clubs, Evertonians saying that if Hickson went, they would go with him, and Kopites responding that if Hickson signed, they would never support the Reds again. His debut for the Reds went like a dream, considering the pressure he was under replacing Billy Liddell in the side, he scored both goals in a 2-1 win over Aston Villa, his first a classic Hickson diving header.

His first love remained Everton and he was a true centre forward in the tradition of Dean and Lawton. He will always be remembered as player of passion and courage, perhaps his own summing up of his career says it all; "I never thought I was a dirty player. I loved the game and I loved getting goals and making goals. Probably I was over-enthusiastic at times, but that's how I played my game. I only knew one way to play, flat out".

Classic Hickson action.

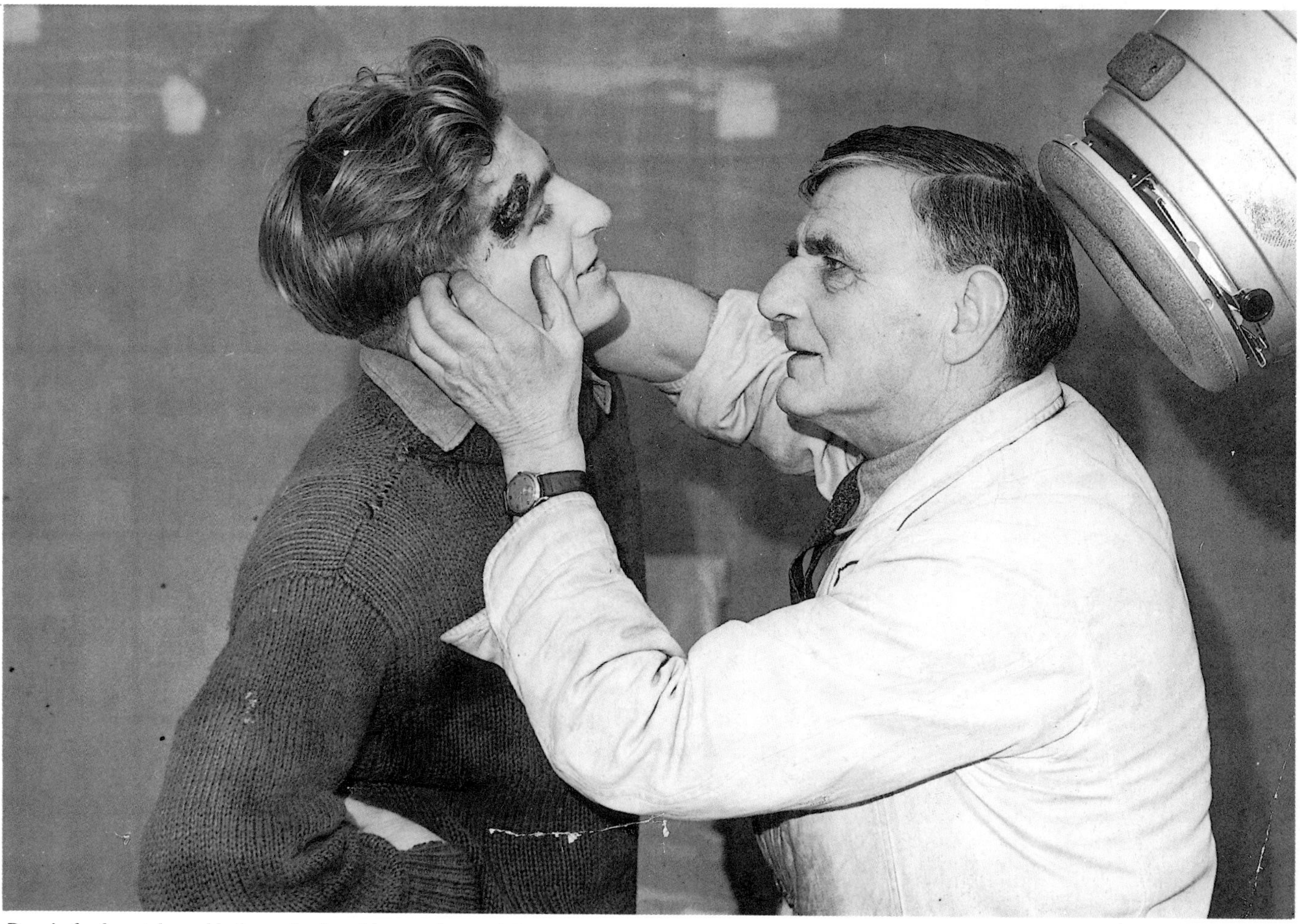

Dave's fearless style could always lead to this sort of nasty injury.

Oglet beach.

OUR DAY OUT

In the early days of the last century, Scousers didn't have to travel very far to get to the seaside, they lived there. The waters of the Mersey and the Irish Sea mingled with a purity that was famed across the North West. Liverpool once rivalled Blackpool as a place "of considerable resort". It was noted for the quality of its bathing, and vast numbers of visitors came in the summer to enjoy "this salubrious and gratifying exercise."

A historian's account of the shore in the region of today's Prince's Dock makes the mind boggle; "The sand was hard and smooth, with a most gentle descent from high to low water, giving no fear for bathers; and though the shore was most frequented at high water, there was nothing to hinder bathers from indulging in their healthy ablutions at any state of the tide."

Further north, past the mile-end rocks, so called because they were a mile from the Town Hall, were two public houses — Breckell's and Bullen's and near to Townsend Mill some cabins on the shore which allegedly "contributed little to the education or morality of the youth of that period."

More historical accounts make the city sound more like a Club 18-30 holiday to Benidorm, than the Liverpool we know today. "There were tents at Bullen's and Breckell's for

drinking, fiddling and dancing; and drunkenness prevailed everywhere; all the streets about Denison Street, Old Hall Street and Great Howard Street were filled with lodgers from the inland towns, who benefited little from their immersions in the river, through their excesses in eating and drinking."

Travelling north from the Liverpool shore our intrepid bather arrived at Bootle, which was another popular resort, particularly in the area of Bootle Castle or Miller's Castle as it was more correctly known. The building, a castellated stone mansion, had been built by a Liverpool solicitor called William Spurstow Miller in 1824, it gave its name to Miller's Bridge.

The last stretch of sandy bathing beach within the Liverpool boundary was at Oglet near Speke airport. This 400 year old one-time village was cut off from the rest of Speke when the airport's 7,500ft runway was built in the Sixties. Gradually, the cottages where shrimpers and the fishermen who harvested the salmon from the clear waters of the Mersey had lived, fell into disrepair. The kids stopped cycling down to the beach with their cozzies and towels, even the courting couples stopped parking their cars in the lane at night, and Oglet died.

New Brighton Pool, May 1952.

IN THE SWIM

For centuries, the British were a filthy nation. The Romans had introduced the habit of bathing into Britain, but unfortunately their public baths became notorious as haunts of vice and debauchery, the early Christians condemned them as places of the Devil and bathing went out of fashion for over a thousand years (the smell on mediaeval Merseyside must have been quite something). Public bathing came back into fashion in the late Eighteenth Century, and the onset of the Industrial Revolution made it a necessity.

The first public baths to be owned by Liverpool Corporation was the tidal bath at the Pier Head, which was purchased from a private company in 1794 at a cost of £4,000. There were ladies' and gents' pools, each one measuring 33ft by 30ft, and a number of private baths where bathers could immerse themselves in warm salt water.

The most remarkable local baths was, however, the Floating Bath. It was promoted by Egerton Smith and Thomas Coglan and constructed in a shipyard at the bottom of Denison Street, being launched on June 11th, 1816.

It was first moored opposite George's Pier, but increasing river traffic caused it to be moved, first to Prince's Pier and then to Wallasey Pool. The historian W. G. Herdman described the baths thus: "the bottom of the bath had an incline from three to seven feet, and across the centre was a passage dividing the deep from the shallow end. The bath was 80 feet long by 27 feet wide and had a constant current of water passing through it.

"There were dressing rooms and a saloon with a large deck which formed a delightful lounge. Here on a calm summer evening, many of the choice spirits of the town assembled, and might be seen quaffing the social glass . . and enjoying the fragrant weed, as they watched the lingering sunset on the Cheshire shore, or noted the occasional daring of some skilful swimmer who leapt from the top of the bath into the river."

The most popular local baths was the large salt-water swimming baths on St. George's Parade at the Pier Head. It was built in 1828 and demolished during the building work at the Pier Head in 1906. The walk between the baths and the river was a regular meeting place for unemployed dockers and seamen. There were many well-worn 'ollie' pitches and lost marbles frequently fouled the baths' suction pumps.

In February 1852 the Council appointed a Committee to manage the baths and wash-houses, there were only four establishments at the time — the Pier Head Baths opened in 1828, Frederick Street Baths and Wash-House in 1842, Paul Street Baths and Wash-House in 1846 and Cornwallis Street Baths in 1851. We might assume that the men who built up this pioneering and highly successful public amenity, must have been some kind of Victorian yuppies, or possibly 'Palmerston's children'. But the *Pen and Ink Sketches*, from the Liverpool Mercury of 1857, convey a different impression of some of the councillors: Thomas Wagstaff (Chairman) . . . Mr. Wagstaff is a hatter in St. James' Street. He is a ruddy good-humoured, fifty years old, and is much respected for his unobtrusive yet somewhat frank manners . . . he is no orator, but merely a plain man, possessing a fair amount of commonsense.''

Samuel Mellor . . . This gentleman is a South American merchant. He is one of the silent members, indeed we do not remember ever having heard the walls of the Municipal Chamber echo to the sound of his voice . . . he is a member of the Finance Committee — for what peculiar qualifications we have never been able to discover''. J. R. McGuffie . . . ''Who can amuse a company, like this portly councillor? He is a chemist, well-known to fame. He is naturally disinclined to speak, and gives as reason that 'there are talkers enough.' . . . he is about fifty years of age, and verifies the old proverb — ''laugh and grow fat.''

John Gladstone Jnr . . . ''Not being gifted with much fluency of speech and being naturally of a retiring disposition, Mr. Gladstone is not qualified to take an active part in public debates . . . not a brilliant man.''

Thomas Fleming . . . ''A tall, ruddy-faced man, somewhat bald and hoary, in a suit of black, walks from the door of the Council Chamber to a seat near the fire-place, throws himself into a chair and after apparently listening attentively to all the proceedings, walks out again . . . we have never heard the sound of his voice.''

Richard Gardner . . . ''He is one of our most successful tradesmen, having realised a handsome fortune. He has a weak voice, lacks nerve and confidence, and when he rises to speak, a timidity or nervous anxiety to acquit himself satisfactorily appears to choke his utterance . . . he is of a happy, kindly, unsuspecting nature.''

All round a fine body of men.

One of the first jobs of the Committee was to sort out the troublesome labour force, it is not surprising they were troublesome, since they worked a 106 hour week for 24s 6d. Pilfering at the baths goes back a long way. In 1857 it was reported that ''following complaints of bathers being robbed at the Pier Head Baths, the superintendent kept watch and by means of marked money, caught the youth responsible. He was taken before the Magistrate and was sentenced to fourteen days in prison, after which term he was sent to the reform ship Akbar for five years.

For more than half a century the Committee vigorously opposed mixed bathing. In September 1871 they even refused permission for a lady swimmer to appear in a gala. Eventually, in September 1887, the first ladies' gala was held in Liverpool, but, with the stipulation that the only male spectators could be parents and elderly male friends of the competitors. After numerous rows in the Council, family

Exciting action at Southport Pool, 1934.

New Brighton Pool, August 1955.

The last dip at Cornwallis Street.

bathing was permitted in April 1914 (was that because most of the men were busy doing something else?). Mixed bathing was first allowed during the summer months only in 1921, and then only at a limited number of baths. It was allowed all year round from 1932.

First Class and Second Class bathing disappeared after the Second World War. There were two classes because the baths had traditionally used the 'Fill and Empty' system. With this method the bath was filled with fresh water, normally at the beginning of the week. Fresh water day was First Class day. When the water became dirty — that was Second Class day. Needless to say such unhygenic methods are not used today.

At one time the City had four free open-air baths for children, these were — Mansfield Street, Gore Street, Burlington Street, and Green Lane which was the only one to survive the Blitz.

The last link with the old baths was severed in December 1967 when Cornwallis Street Baths was closed. A mere shadow of their former glory they had gradually fallen into disrepair since being damaged during the Second World War. One Scouseologist recalls his trips there with the school, "it had segregated pools for men and women, and the salt water was always bitingly cold. The water was drawn from an underground chamber at the Pier Head adjacent to the old George's Baths. The chambers filled with water as the tide came in, it was then allowed to settle and subsequently pumped via an underground pipeline to Cornwallis Street, (no wonder it tasted foul)". The baths with their cubicles without doors, relaxed attitude to bathing attire, ("cozzies, undies or in the nude, pal"), peeling paintwork, and general feeling of seediness that only something that was once truly beautiful but has now decayed can give, are light years away from the warm fun pools of today with their spouting whales, wave machines and mock tropical islands.

The old baths certainly had their appeal; diving for stones you'd picked up between the tramlines on the way there, depth charging your mates, Brylcreem machines, eyeing up the girls, red eyes from swimming underwater looking for those stupid stones; and a taste in your mouth like you'd been gargling with Chloros. Given a choice between the old and the new, We know which we'd choose. Give us the plastic palms any day!

THE SPORTS CENTRE SET

When Mrs. Dorene Lyon of Walton took her daughters Lorraine aged 7 and Samantha aged 8 along to the Everton Park sports centre in 1982, it was simply to pass some time during the children's half term holiday. When she gave them instructions to play on the trampoline she was unaware that both girls were to display an extraordinary amount of natural talent. So much so, that by 1988 Lorraine was to become a world age group champion and with much of her potential still to be realised, is likely to become a winner of major titles in the future. Lorraine's other interests include gymnastics, swimming, morris dancing, drawing and writing.

Fazakerley's Alex Kruger was working at a Hemel Hempstead sports centre, when he heard he had been chosen to accompany the great Daley Thompson as Britain's decathlon representatives, in the Seoul Olympics. A member of the Liverpool Pembroke Athletics Club, Alex was sponsored by Liverpool City Council and the Liverpool Echo.

BILLY HOOLE

In 1910 a young teacher at St. Polycarp's school in Great Homer Street, who was waiting in his classroom for his evening classes to start, noticed a group of youngsters hanging about in the rain outside the school, showing no interest in going home. Billy Hoole, the young teacher recently arrived in Liverpool from his home town of Doncaster, took pity on the children and invited them back into the school.

Billy knew what their home life was like, it was little more than an existence in the slums that passed for homes in that area in early days of the century. Sometimes there were families of over twenty packed into a filthy five or six room house, most had very little sanitation much less anywhere to play. Very often children could not get in when they got home, mothers almost inevitably worked long hours and fathers were frequently drunk.

So Billy Hoole collected papers, paints, crayons, unwanted games from friends, in fact anything that could be considered useful and the first Play Centre was born. This was yet another first for Merseyside, and the idea soon spread across the country. Margaret Beavan and Florence Melly were enthusiastic supporters of the scheme in the city, and the second centre, known as the Children's Happy Evening Centre opened in Penrhyn Street School shortly afterwards. The teachers gave their time free and were backed up by teams of volunteers. For a few hours each schoolday evening, ragged schoolgirls sat and sewed or painted, while the local 'scallies' boxed and played games (or was it the other way round?).

By the outbreak of the First World War, the scheme was operating on a city-wide basis. During the war years the Play Centres virtually disappeared but in 1919 they were revived when the City Council started paying teachers for running them. In 1920, the Holiday Games in the Parks programme was started by the Education Committee, and in 1929 school playgrounds were opened as Summer Play Centres.

The 1939 evacuation ended all three schemes. Then the Ministry of Labour and National Service, wanting more women for the factories, asked local authorities to make

provision for children after school hours while their mothers were still at work. So Play Centres were opened en-masse five evenings a week from 4 to 6 p.m. for all ages of children. Teachers worked a rota as child minders during holidays and on Saturdays.

After the war, the Play Centres were re-launched and continued in one guise or another into the Sixties.

The last word on Play Centres should rightly belong to Billy Hoole, the man who started it all; "Everyone is busy finding out why children become juvenile criminals. Boredom, sheer boredom is the reason." Recalling those far-off days, he remembers the streets around St. Polycarp's where his children lived; "They faced intolerable conditions but there was a spirit in the slums. Anyone ill or in trouble and the whole street was there. You don't find that wonderful spirit today in the suburbs".

ADVENTURE

In April 1954, Liverpool was offered the opportunity to become the first provincial city to experiment with adventure playgrounds. Funded by the National Playing Fields Association, the idea was to provide places where children could have the freedom to indulge in constructive play, the materials in the playground would be old motor cars, bricks, pieces of wood, in fact anything that could be used imaginatively.

One of the prime movers in Liverpool was the legendary H. S. Magnay, whose name appeared on so many school documents that it was burned into the memory of tens of thousands of scouse schoolkids growing up in the post-war years. Magnay was Director of Education, but his involvement in playground development came through his role as head of the Liverpool Juvenile Delinquency Committee, which was charged with keeping young people off the streets, or at least if they were on them, to keep them on the straight and narrow ones.

The first adventure playground was in Rathbone Street in the shadow of Liverpool Cathedral but it was not without problems. Miss Joyce Ellis, the first full-time play leader, returned from lunch one day to find her star piece of equipment, an old Austin coupe, being transported away in

pieces on a handcart. Motor vehicles and motor parts were at a premium at that time and the next vehicle, a Vauxhall shooting brake, had to have a round the clock guard, one prospective mechanic came from Hightown having seen a picture of the car in the Liverpool Echo, he needed a replacement carburettor for his own Vauxhall.

The Victoria Settlement adventure playground in 1959.

Whitley Gardens, Shaw Street, 1960.

PLAY STREETS

For most Liverpool youngsters, the street was the only playground they knew. In 1948 many streets were made safer by the City Council implementing the Street Playgrounds Act of 1938. Play streets were officially described as "streets closed to vehicular traffic between the hours of sunrise and sunset, unless the vehicles are calling at houses in the street." The streets had the desired effect, road accidents decreased and children were free to play kick-the-can, kingie, statues, jacks or just poke sticks into tar bubbles in those summer streets of childhood.

UNCLE KEN

At first sight, Ken Clarke was a real eccentric, a Salvador Dali style waxed moustache, the artist's goatee beard, a long stemmed pipe and a Left Bank beret. But Ken, who was one of Liverpool's pioneering play leaders in the early sixties, was only eccentric in that many of his ideas were ahead of his time. He recognised the problems caused by the demolition of the old inner areas of the city and the subsequent move into high rise flats, and sought a novel solution to the vexed question of 'Where are the children going to play?'

Ken's answer was simple and reached fulfilment in the Grenville Street adventure playground off Great George Street in 1964. 140 tons of rubble from demolished slum dwellings were brought to a patch of waste land in Grenville Street, the rubble was dumped in mounds, and tons of concrete poured over the rough shapes making concrete mountains with slides and tunnels, hollows which became paddling pools and sand pits, and amazingly an open-air community theatre. The whole project took Ken 2½ years with the help of student volunteers who came from all over the world to help in their vacations.

Ken who moved on from Liverpool in 1965 was Mr. Perpetual Motion, he survived on only 4 hours sleep a night, he had been a councillor in Cheshire and in Worcestershire, and had only ever taken one holiday in his life, having devoted all his spare time to community work.

When the children who used the playground found out that Uncle Ken was leaving, they raised money to buy him a watch by making and selling lemonade. Uncle Ken went off in search of fresh challenges but his legacy remained in the pleasure his work gave to thousands of youngsters who played with imagination and safety thanks to his vision.

THE GREENBANK PROJECT

Gerry Kinsella is not a name that springs immediately to mind when discussing Merseyside's sporting greats but Gerry's achievements rank with anybody's and exceed many. Gerry Kinsella, a polio victim, is disabled but his sporting prowess in paraplegic games is legendary. He has won international gold medals in swimming, basketball, wheelchair marathons and javelin throwing. He has raised thousands of pounds for the physically handicapped in Liverpool by completing marathon wheelchair pushes between John O'Groats and Lands End and from Liverpool to Hamburg. Toxteth's Gerry worked with the Manpower Services Commission to set up the Greenbank Project, a unique scheme based at the former Greenbank school in Mossley Hill, which assists the disabled to develop work skills and integrate them into the community. The project has been responsible for the setting up of a special factory in Speke and the launch of a monthly newspaper — The Greenbank World. In 1988 Gerry and colleague Vincent Ross developed a revolutionary three wheeled chair which made its first official appearance at the Asda Mersey Marathon, on September 25th. It is hoped that wheelchairs made in Speke can be exported throughout the world.

Gerry Kinsella.

THE GREAT SHOWMAN

In July 1982, the face of Napoleon Bonaparte was seen at Litherland Town Hall. The bronze death mask of the French Emperor — one of only two in the world — was on display at an antiques fair. It belonged to Don Ellis, the Liverpool impresario. It had been given to his great uncle by Leopold, King of the Belgians, for his work as a mosaic artist, and had been passed down through the family.

The bronze cast was one of the two made by Doctor Autommarchi from impressions taken after Napoleon's death in 1821. The other hangs over Napoleon's tomb in Les Invalides in Paris. It was the first time for more than 40 years that the mask had been on public view on Merseyside. On the previous occasion, it was displayed in the foyer of the old Paramount cinema in London Road, when they were showing 'Napoleon and Josephine.'

Originally an impressionist, Don Ellis devoted most of his working life to keeping music hall alive. His Old Time Music Hall at the Floral Pavilion, New Brighton was legendary, and ran for 28 consecutive years until Don's death in 1984, following a brave fight against cancer. On the opening night of his last Music Hall he said; ''Show business is my life — I hope to go on for a number of years.'' Two months later Don Ellis was dead. In 1985 a plaque was unveiled at the Floral Pavilion in memory of this real 'trooper.'

The young Don Ellis. Could this pic have been taken at Jerome's?

Don Ellis pictured in 1976.

Don with stars of a Liverpool Empire Music Hall show in 1971. Reg Dixon, Kim Cordell, Don, Sandy Powell and Cavan O'Connor.

Don in 1961 with Kenny Baker.

MY BOOMERANG WON'T COME BACK

In the summer of 1868, Australia's first sporting tourists were on Merseyside. The Aboriginal cricket team were playing at Bootle. The Aboriginals had quite a respectable record on the tour, winning 47 matches, losing 14 and drawing 19.

The after match entertainment was almost as much an attraction as the cricket. The players donned costumes of possum skin and lyre bird feathers to engage in mock battles or to throw weapons called kangaroo rats. There were also exhibitions of boomerang throwing, running backwards for 100 yards, and dodging the cricket ball. One particular player, Dick-a-Dick was the star of these exhibitions. Armed only with a club and a small shield, he would challenge three men to throw cricket balls at him simultaneously from 15 yards. He was only hit twice on the whole tour, and the public acclaim resulting from his dexterity and agility resulted in his club being preserved in the Lord's cricket museum.

Bootle was the most notable stop on the tour for a rather unfortunate reason, Mullagh the star player, was guilty of a wayward throw with a boomerang, killing a spectator in the crowd.

Surely another first for Merseyside.

THE WHISPERERS IN THE DARKNESS

In publishers' parlance, Clive Barker is 'hot'. The Quarry Bank lad who presented mime shows at the Everyman Theatre with the Mute Pantomime Theatre, The Dog Troop, and later spent a total of nine years on the dole is 'hot' indeed. During his doleful years, Clive passed his time writing plays and short stories until success beckoned with a series of horror stories published under the collective title of 'Clive Barker's Books of Blood,' they were an enormous hit in the horror market, particularly in the U.S.A. More success followed with the publication of his first novel "The Damnation Game". Enough for your average scouse lad you may think, but average our Clive certainly is not.

Next off the Barker conveyor belt was a horror movie which he wrote and directed himself, 'Hellraiser'. Anyone who is a regular visitor to video shops will know this, it's one with the disgusting sleeve where people wander around with their skins apparently turned inside out. His latest movie 'The Hellbound Heart' looks likely to cement his reputation as a film maker, and the advance from his publisher for his latest book, 'Weaveworld', a fantasy set in Liverpool, will keep his bank manager smiling for the foreseeable future. In between times Clive found time to write a West End play, 'The Secret Life of Cartoons', a comedy in which an animator comes home to find his cartoon character, Rosco the Rabbit, in bed with his wife.

Clive, born in Oakdale Road off Penny Lane in 1952, had his fascination for horror writing stimulated as a schoolboy, when Ramsey Campbell went along to his school to give a talk on the literature of the macabre.

Campbell, who was born in Wavertree Garden Suburb in 1946, is well known to many locals as the film critic for Radio Merseyside, but his international reputation is as a writer of macabre stories. This one-time tax inspector and librarian had his first story 'The Room in the Castle' published when he was only 16.

While Clive Barker's success has been spectacularly sudden, Ramsey's has been a steady climb to reach his present position of eminence in his field. Much of his work is based in Liverpool, and novels like 'The Doll Who Ate His Mother', 'The Face That Must Die', and 'The Parasite' helped enhance his reputation. In 1987 'Dark Feasts' was published, a volume celebrating Ramsey Campbell's 25 years of writing.

He has won numerous awards, and his book covers are freely littered with quotes like: "Easily the best horror writer working in Britain today", and "Campbell writes the most terrifying horror tales of anyone alive today".

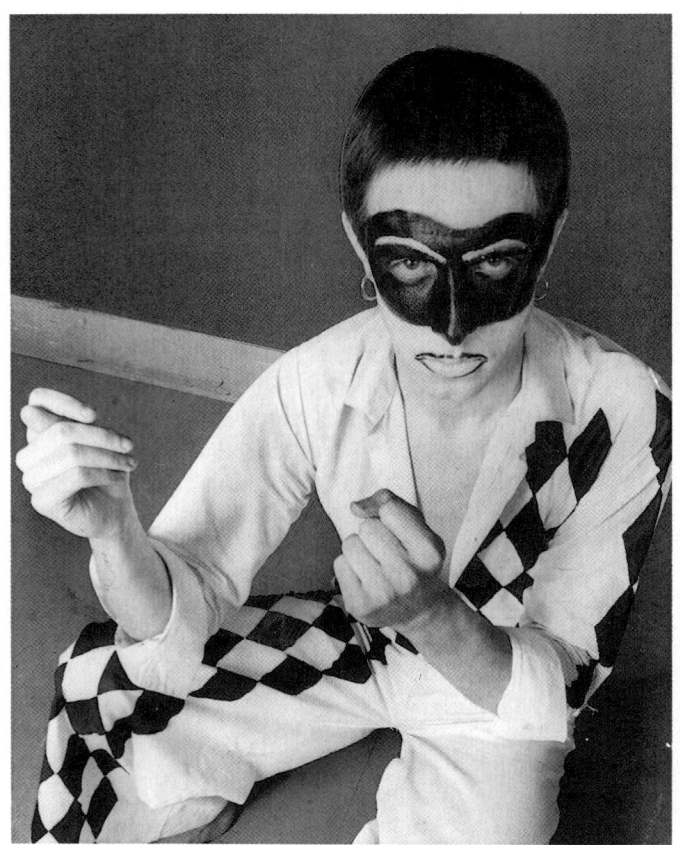

Barker in 1976 and 1987.

Campbell in 1976 and 1987.

FIRST OF THE BAD MEN

He would enter the ring to a deafening chorus of boos, his hair, soon to be an unruly mass, was swept back, long, black and sleek as a bat's wing, away from the rugged face, his features impassive except for an occasional sneer or even a snarl if one of the ringside insults was hurtful enough. His dressing gown discarded, the barrel-chested man in the long black tights moved menacingly towards his opponent. Friday night at the Stadium, Jack Pye topping the bill.

Jack Pye did more than any other man to put wrestling on the map in Britain. He was the man the fans loved to hate, although everybody knew that among the boos, catcalls and occasional swipes with umbrellas and handbags as he left the ring, there was real affection for the man and it was all part of the game.

Although he was known in his early days as the Doncaster Panther he was actually born in Hindley, near Wigan. He was a miner's son and went to the same village school as the young George Formby. He went down the pit himself until he became part of the legendary Wigan wrestling fraternity of the twenties with performers such as Norm the Butcher, King Kong Curtis and Billy Riley. Riley was reckoned to be the most skilful wrestler ever produced by Wigan and in the summer of 1933 a crowd of 25,000 saw an epic battle between Pye and Riley at the local football stadium.

Pye's professional career got under way at the King's Hall, Belle Vue, in 1929, and by the time the Stadium opened its doors to wrestling in 1933, Jack was already a big star. He thrilled the crowds with bouts against some of the great wrestlers of the day, Chick Knight, Sam Radnor and the World Champion Jim Londos, the "Golden Greek." In 1957 he took on another World Champion at the Stadium. Lou Thesz from the U.S.A., reckoned to be one of the all-time Greats. Possibly his best remembered contest was when he defeated and unmasked the American wrestler the Zebra Kid in front of a sell-out Stadium crowd.

He continued to pack the fans in during the dark days of war, and in one notable contest was thrown out of the ring narrowly missing a 20ft deep crater caused by Hermann Goering when he tried a body smash on Jack from 5,000 ft, but missed the ring completely.

Bruised kidneys forced Pye's retirement in 1963, after more than 5,000 contests it came as no surprise. In February 1964 he made his last appearance at the Stadium when John Moores, in his capacity as managing director of Liverpool Stadium, presented Jack with a pair of diamond-studded cuff links to mark his retirement. Apart from a brief come-back in 1971, when he beat the Masked Destroyer at Liverpool's Top Rank Suite followed by a couple of other bouts and a few guest appearances as referee, Jack lived the life of a successful Lancashire businessman running a night club, casino and gymnasium in his adopted home town, Blackpool.

Jack Pye died in December 1985, the gentle giant who became the first, and greatest, of the badmen.

Jack Pye with Sir John Moores. Jack is on the left.

Kirkdale Recreation Ground, the gallows was situated in the top left of the ground.

HANG 'EM HIGH

When you sit in your car on Scotland Road, stuck in a traffic jam of like-minded individuals heading north to worship at the temples of Anfield and Goodison, you are following in the footsteps the 40,000 and 50,000 crowds of yesteryear who flocked to Liverpool's best attended 'entertainment'; the public executions at Kirkdale Gaol.

Kirkdale Gaol was built between 1821 and 1822, it closed in 1891 and was bought by Liverpool Corporation. The buildings were demolished and the site passed over to the Parks and Gardens department in 1897. Tons of earth were brought in to cover the site, and it was laid out with gardens and bowling greens. The only visible reminder of the site's original purpose was the prison's bronze bell that stood on a plinth near the entrance to the park in Sessions Road. Unfortunately the bell was stolen from a corporation storage yard in 1946.

Initially the prison was just a local jail, but in 1835 it was designated as a place of execution. The first public hanging was on August 28th, 1835, when James Barlow from Hindley near Wigan, was executed for the murder of his wife. A crowd of about 50,000, many from as far as Preston gathered in the late morning, barefoot children and shawlies mingled with members of the local gentry, and everywhere the ever-present thieves and pickpockets, one old man from St. Helens told a reporter from the Liverpool Mercury that fear of pickpockets had made him leave his watch and chain at home,

and only bring sufficient funds with him to get to Kirkdale and then home.

The grisly spectacle may be repugnant to us today, but all punishments were hard in those days. During the 1823 Easter hearings at the Sessions House, which stood adjacent to the prison, one poor unfortunate from Ormskirk was sentenced to transportation for the theft of two silver salt spoons, as was a Liverpool man found guilty of stealing a hat.

The most celebrated public hanging at Kirkdale was that of Captain Henry Rogers in September 1857. Rogers had sadistically and systematically tortured a crewman to death during a trip by the 'Martha Jane' from Barbados to Liverpool. Rogers was only brought to book by the courage of some members of the Martha Jane's crew in going to the police when the ship docked in Liverpool. This was one of the few occasions when a sea captain was brought to justice for brutality to his crew. Within four days of the execution a waxwork model of Rogers was on display in the Chamber of Horrors at Mr. Alsopp's Crystal Palace in Lime Street, wearing Rogers' own clothes purchased from Calcraft, the hangman.

Public executions were abolished in 1868, and as one contemporary writer put it: "At last the cries of the condemned will no longer be drowned by the catcalls and mockery of a vulgar crowd that includes the very dregs of society."

It could be the only time Ray Clemence 'scored' at Anfield. As usual the play is at the other end.

Liverpool's British ice dance champions of the late sixties and early seventies, Susan Getty and Roy Bradshaw. Susan from Townsend Lane and Roy from Eastbourne Road, Aintree came fourth in the world championships of 1971. Susan, a former telex operator at Plessey's and Roy, a cook at Henderson's restaurant married in 1971 and emigrated to Canada where they became skating coaches in Ontario.

World non-stop skating record holder Billy Wetherall about to attempt another record at the Ritz Roller Rink in 1933. Dom Volante is cutting the tape.

Now what's all this? Two leading Liverpudlian journalists demonstrating the new sport of synchronised reporting? No, it can't be that — the smiles aren't wide enough. Perhaps our two intrepid reporters are following up rumours of a nose dive into a Liverpool fountain. Has Professor Codman been forced to go underwater? Was Esther Williams from Liverpool? She may have been, but we're sure she didn't wear specs when swimming and a certain Louis B. Mayer wouldn't have approved the nose . . . Well, he might have. No, it's suspense time again. To find out exactly what our two punch drunk reporters are up to, turn to page 122.

REYNOLDS' WAXWORKS

At the turn of the century, Liverpool's favourite place of entertainment was not one of the many music halls dotted around the city but a three storey building on Lime Street carrying the name Reyonlds' Exhibition. Popularly known as Reynolds' Waxworks, the building had originally been built as a masonic hall, but a last minute hitch in negotiations between the builders and the lodge concerned allowed local businessman, Alfred Reynolds, to come in and snap up the lease. Reynolds, a skilled modeller, as was his son Charles, opened the waxworks in 1854 as Reynolds' "Gallery of Illustrations". Business boomed, and in 1876 Alfred Reynolds bought the building outright and made extensive alterations.

By this time it was known as Reynolds' Exhibition and had many other attractions as well as wax models, there were performing animals, stage performances by singers, illusionists and variety acts of all kinds, and most popular of all, a Christmas pantomime performed by wooden marionettes.

In the early days the whole of the top floor was devoted to an enormous tableau. "Life on the Liverpool Landing Stage", with skilful scene painting and use of wax figures, a *diorama* of 500 characters was achieved. As with all waxworks the Chamber of Horrors was one of the most enduring attractions, and after visitors had passed through the gallery of poisoners, stranglers and axemen they entered the entertainment section. Some of the slower witted

customers failed to notice the transition and on seeing the scowling portrayal of Richard II by the great actor Barry Sullivan would ask the attendant "Who did *he* murder?", the laconic reply was given "Shakespeare".

Although live performers such as Karnak the Conjuror, Mystic Muriel, the Sisters Fay and Madame Tesla (The Women with the X-Ray Eyes) were great attractions, for many visitors the stars of the show were the animals. The first animals appeared in 1865, the publicity material referred to them as "performing fish" and "Educated Monsters of the Deep", but we know them better as seals. The keeper who looked after them was an imposing figure, draped in gold braid, looking like some Ruritanian general, he was known to the local wags as the Lord High Privy Seal.

Always popular were Madame Eichlerette's monkeys, with stars like Koko and Kokotina who did a double act, "Tourists on Honeymoon", Jojo, a chimpanzee who used to catch a rubber ball fired from a cannon, and Ski-hi who made a balloon ascent to the top of the auditorium, then bailed out into the audience using a parachute, while he was on high he would take off all his clothes causing the ladies in the audience below to shriek, and modestly cover their eyes, well, almost cover them.

Professor Peterson's Troupe of Canine Comedians featured a poodle dog who was billed as a female impersonator, he played the widow in a canine drama entitled "Thomas Atkins or She Wiped Away a Tear." The real doggy star was,

however, Bow-wowski the Dog Pianist, it was said that as a puppy he showed such musical potential that he was sent away to the Conservatoire at Leipzig.

There were two professors in the Faculty of Performing Fleas, an Italian, Professor Urbino, and an Englishman with the patriotic name of Professor England. Urbino gave a mock scientific show, exhibiting his entomological subjects on white tables and giving a Professor Bronowski style presentation of his subjects. England was altogether more of a showman, he made elaborate props and sets for his performers, his pièce-de-résistance being a church with lighted windows and a tiny hearse drawn by six fleas which solemnly made its way down a narrow path to the fleas' cemetery.

Without doubt the greatest attraction at Reynolds', and one which made the most lasting impression on those who saw him, was the lion-headed boy. Looking remarkably like Lon Chaney Jnr. as the wolfman, he would wander around the exhibition dressed in a Little Lord Fauntleroy black velvet suit with a white lace collar. His name was Steve, and assuring visitors not to be afraid he would invite them to feel his hand and pull his hair, ''I am quite human'', he would say.

In spite of its popularity the march of time could not be resisted and in 1922 Reynolds' closed its doors for the last time, beaten by those new-fangled silent movies.

The final chapter in the Reynolds' story was played out in March 1923 when the contents of the exhibition went under the auctioneer's hammer.

Sadly most of the models were valued more for the clothes they stood in, and the plate glass cases that surrounded them, than for the skill of the modellers' craft which formed them.

The Kaiser directing the destruction of Rheims Cathedral fetched £2 6s, Burke and Hare 17s, Mrs. Maybrick 16s and Henry VIII and his wives £24 13s 6d, doubtless for the fine garments which adorned them. The spectacular Sleeping Beauty, who did her mechanical breathing inside a handsome glass case fetched a laudable fifteen guineas. Dr. Crippen was sold for 24s to find honourable employment as a tailor's dummy. One wonders did he stand, glassy-eyed in a draper's window somewhere in town wearing somebody's ''Five Guinea Non Pareil Suit'' or possibly something, ''Perfect for that Long Sea Voyage''. Ah well, that's entertainment.

The Lion Boy.

Reynolds' tableaux.

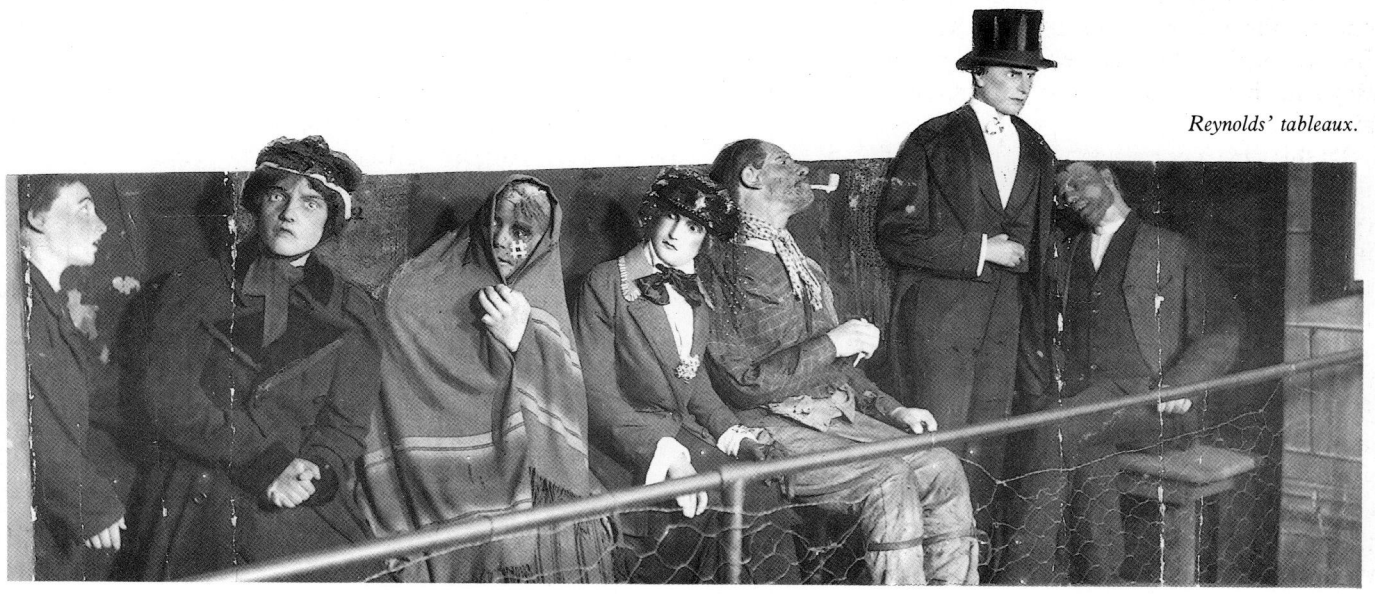

BATTER UP

Baseball on Merseyside goes back almost as far as football. It was certainly in existence here before the Football League was formed in 1888, though in those far-off days it was more akin to rounders, indeed some of the clubs were known as rounders teams. Union and West Derby rounders clubs were among the best known.

It was around 1892 that the rules, and the name, were changed over to baseball, and after the First World War strenuous attempts were made to popularise the sport, but cricket retained its grip as the premier summer game.

The rules of the English Baseball Association were drawn up by Mr. W. H. Hivey, who was the last of the hereditary freemen of Liverpool.

The big event on the English baseball calendar is the regular international played between England and Wales. The English EBA clubs are clustered around Liverpool, while the Welsh clubs are all in the Cardiff and Newport area. In the pre-war days, thousands used to watch the games on the old Edinburgh Park ground, but today 100 would be a big crowd.

American baseball, a different game from the English variety, has all but disappeared from the local sporting scene. The days when Goodison Park echoed to the raucous cries of thousands of gum-chewing, crew-cutted American servicemen are long gone. In the glory days, immediately before, during and after the war, crowds of over 10,000 were commonplace. The U.S. airbase at Burtonwood provided a steady stream of talent to play for local clubs, as well as putting their own teams in the competitions. The 'Nitestics', the base's military policemen, were one of the most successful sides of the post-war era.

Interest in the American game was stimulated by a tour of Britain in 1924 by the New York Giants and the Chicago White Sox, who played an exhibition game at Goodison Park, the plate was at the Park end of the ground and several of the biggest hits took the ball clear over the Goodison Park stand.

The sport was encouraged by John Moores during the 1930's. Before Australian football was introduced to our coupons, he desperately wanted to fill the gap during the league's summer break. Since baseball scores are often similar to those of soccer, he planned a summer system based on baseball. To help him in this, he imported some of the top American and Canadian stars to work in his business. The scheme never took off as a commercial proposition, but the sport became very popular at an amateur level.

Many local footballers played baseball, the Everton footballers even raised their own side. Dixie Dean was an excellent player, as was Liverpool's Lance Carr, who played for Liverpool Giants, while at Anfield, and for Blackpool Seagulls after he left the Reds. Carr was a South African who had arrived in Liverpool along with Berry Niewenhuys, better remembered as 'Nivvy', in 1933.

During the Giants/White Sox tour, the match at Stamford Bridge was watched by George Bernard Shaw, who made the following pithy comment about sport.

"It is a noteworthy fact that kicking and beating have played such a part in the habits which necessity has imposed on mankind in past ages, that the only way of preventing civilised men from kicking and beating their wives is to organise games, in which they can kick and beat balls."

Union rounders team 1888.

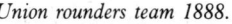

THE WALNUT

The early sixties was a time of great expansion in the further education system, but the march of progress always leaves casualties.

When Liverpool University was building its new Department of Mathematics, an integral part of student life fell victim to the bulldozer. "Mrs. Mac's", otherwise known as the Walnut Hotel, was the student's pub. Its nickname had come through the long reign of a motherly manageress of the fifties. What made the Walnut unique was the ceiling of the small, panelled smoke-room. On the ceiling the students had recorded their names in pencil and lipstick for years. Looking at the ceiling, the demolition men must have wondered, who was "Hot Rod Simmons", or who was John of "Who says Big John can't hold his ale", fame.

Many of the scribblers went on to make their mark elsewhere. When the ceiling had been repainted for the last time, among the names obliterated had been the late Mr. Justice Lynskey and Rose Heilbron. The re-painting had been carried out during the summer vacation, on the students' return there was a near riot.

Inside the Walnut, 1958.

LIFE WITH THE LIONS

A zoo keeper at Liverpool Zoo in 1937 read Rex his bedtime story. 'Born Free' maybe . . .

THE LITTLE PEOPLE

A one line entry in the Second Whitbread Book of Scouseology, 'Leprechauns spotted in Jubilee Drive, Liverpool 7,' is the tip of the iceberg of one of the city's most bizarre stories.

On several warm July evenings in 1964 the city's parks were packed with youngsters looking for leprechauns, the centre of attention being Jubilee Park, where scores of police were drafted in to keep traffic moving and control the crowds who trampled through the shrubbery and invaded the bowling greens. Police eventually cleared the bowling greens, closed the Park gates, and stood guard.

Irish Park bobby, James Nolan ("I don't believe in leprechauns myself"), who was wearing a crash helmet to protect himself from stone throwing little people, said at the time: "This all started on Tuesday. How, I just don't know, but the sooner it ends the better. Stones have been thrown onto the bowling green and for the second night running no one has been able to play. The kids just won't go away. Some swear they have seen leprechauns. The story has gone round and now we are beseiged with leprechaun hunters."

One nine-year-old boy was sure he had seen a leprechaun: "Last night I saw little men with white hats throwing stones and sods at each other on the bowling green. Honest, I did."

Gradually the leprechaunomania subsided, and the incidents were passed down into Liverpool folklore, and all but forgotten until 1982, when the Liverpool Echo came up with a World Exclusive . . . they had found the leprechaun, his name was Brian Jones, and this was his story . . .

If my grandfather's garden had not been a wilderness all this would not have happened.

Grandfather's house in Edge Lane had a huge garden, backing on to Kensington Gardens, with a ten-foot high wall hiding the bowling green and park.

I'd promised grandfather to tidy up — a formidable task as the weeds had grown higher than me.

Mind you, I'm a smallish sort of chap. Like most gardeners my gardening gear reflected my past rather than sartorial elegance — well worn navy trousers tucked into my Wellingtons, denim shirt, woollen hat with a red bobble, and an old red waistcoat.

I stood sucking on my empty pipe, pondering my plan of attack on the kitchen garden with its six-foot high weeds. It was a warm, peaceful summer afternoon, and the sunlight was dancing in flickering rays through the leaves.

Suddenly, I heard children's voices whispering. They were sat astride the park wall, looking down into the garden.

One voice croaked, terrified: "It's a leprechaun." Obviously from atop the wall the children did not realise the full height of the weeds. And how much shorter I was!

The boys were from the Roman Catholic school down the road, where there were lots of Irish.

In a flash the idea came to me.

I bounded into view, babbling made-up words, I jumped up and down, picked up turves and threw them at the children.

In blind panic they fell off the wall and ran . . . And by the time I had clambered up to peer over, they were disappearing through the gate on the far side of the bowling green.

Next evening I was back at work in the garden. Over in the park I could hear the sounds of a crowd, something like a football or bowling tournament I thought, and carried on toiling.

But finally inquisitiveness caught me. And I decided to peep over the wall to see what was happening.

I paused to light my pipe, clambered up on an old wheel and peered over, taking in the scene.

For a second or two nothing happened. I saw three hundred or so children standing on the raised water reservoir across the bowling green all facing me.

There was a sudden hush. Followed by a shout: "There he is. There's the leprechaun."

This time I fell off the wall! What if they chased me? I went back to digging . . . apprehensively.

But the children did not follow. They stayed on top of the reservoir. Obviously they must be scared. My sense of humour returned. My confidence too.

I appeared at different parts of the wall and shook my fist, to show them I was no friendly leprechaun.

I threw turves into the air. Each salvo and each appearance brought a roar from the crowd. This went on for an hour.

Then I'd had enough. I changed, and cycled round to the park and joined the children, listening to their boasts. One had seen two leprechauns. Someone, six, and more and more, until there was a whole colony.

The next day, Saturday, there was no school, so I was confident of being undisturbed in the garden. How wrong I was.

When I drove up to grandfather's I found myself pushing through a crowd, not just children, but adults too. All outside grandfather's house.

Finally a policeman arrived at the door. "Have you any idea how this started?" He asked.

Grandfather and I shook our heads.

"If I could find out the bloody idiot who started all this, I would put him away for good," said the policeman.

At eleven o'clock that night the crowd still had not left.

For a week I didn't dare to go back to the garden. But when I eventually did I saw that the children had been in. They had broken into the garden shed. But not dared to brave those thick weeds though.

Gradually they became braver, and in the next two weeks I saw all my work ruined.

It was one evening, some time later, as I was pumping up the tyres of my bike by the front gate that I overheard two boys talking at the bus stop.

The whole school had decided to capture the little people, stick them in jamjars and take them to school to prove to their teachers that they really existed.

They planned to use airguns. At least ten boys had them. I realised I could never again be safe in the garden.

Two days later and I had found a solution. I changed into my leprechaun outfit, as I had come to call it, and went down to an empty house, very similar to my grandfather's about six doors away.

I started my routine. I popped up and down, threw turves . . . everything.

Two more performances on the following nights and the trick had worked.

I was left alone peacefully in grandfather's garden.

But the children took their vengeance on the other garden, and within a fortnight they had destroyed it. Six weeks later and the house was destroyed. The council had to demolish it.

I've never dared to tell the story before . . . but this is it, and no blarney!

● **Footnote:** The house belonging to Brian Jones' grandfather has also been demolished — to make way for premises for the family firm, Dave Jones (Marine).

Brian Jones left Merseyside a few years ago to take up farming in Anglesey.

Published by kind permission of the Liverpool Echo.

THE FUN NEVER SETS ON MERSEYSIDE

The Barrister in the dock robbery case was probing the Docker in the witness box. .

"What kind of gloves were they"?

The Docker stared straight at him.

"They were the kind", he said, "dat you put on yer hands".

Freda and Josie were looking at the Beatles pictures adorning the walls of the Abbey Road pub.

"Ah look," said Josie, "there's poor John".

"He doesn't look too well on that one," replied Freda.

"No, he doesn't, I think that was taken when he went a bit funny. You know, when he ran off with that Ayatola fella".

Billy came home in floods of tears after his first day at Joseph Williams Primary School.

"What's the matter, Son?" his Mum asked.

Billy was upset because his teacher had told lies.

She said sit there for the present and I didn't get anything all day," said Billy.

Remember the hula hoop craze of the late 1950's? Liverpool's Barbara Mitchell and her group the Vernons, demonstrates the technique perfectly in rehearsal for ATV's 'Oh Boy' show in October 1958.

THE FUN NEVER SETS ON MERSEYSIDE

Roy and Ray were in Nottingham to see Everton play at the City ground. Unsure of the way they stopped and asked a policeman the way to the ground. He gave them directions but ten minutes later they found themselves back at the same place with the same policeman. Roy wound down the window ''No wonder you lot couldn't catch Robin Hood'' he shouted at a bemused policeman.

Jim was in Harrow, lost. He stopped a local resident Excuse me, how do you get to Wembley?'

''Beat Liverpool'' was the enlightened Cockney's reply.

W.E.L. Malings of the Warrington Caledonian Society tossing the caber at the Lancashire and Cheshire Scottish Society's field day at the Crawford Athletic Ground in 1951.

YOU SHOULD BE ON THE STAGE, YEAH! I KNOW — THE LANDING STAGE

Panto at the Empire in 1933. Marie Burke as Dick Whittington and a dirty big moggie.

Eleanore Wilson and David Dobell during rehearsal for the Liverpool Playhouse production of "Grouse in June" in December 1939.

Lalla Dodd, the Liverpool born former telephone operator in her role as Aladdin in 1935.

Liverpool's Muriel Cronshaw (a Scouseology favourite — remember her in last year's quiz?) as Robinson Crusoe in 1938.

A glamorous line up for the Royal Court's 1966 production of 'Tom Thumb'.

Shirley Cook as the Good Fairy in Tom Arnold's 'Babes in the Wood' which played the Liverpool Empire in 1951. Stars of the panto were Jewell and Warriss.

"What is it darling — not bad news I pray?".
"Frightfully bad news I'm afraid darling"
"It's not, it's not Reggie is it darling?"
"No darling, it's not Reggie darling, frightfully worse than that I'm afraid darling".
"You mean we've been unlucky in the Wimbledon ticket draw darling?".
"No darling it's not that — far worse darling".
"Tell me darling — be brave darling".
"Brace yourself darling, we've been, oh darling I'm so frightfully sorry — we've been accepted for the 'Hold Your Plums' audience.
"My God!!!!"

The cast of "Four Sided Triangle", Adrienne Corri, Edward Judd, Amanda Reiss and Richard Todd toast the success of the play at the Liverpool Playhouse in 1970.

SHEER CLASS

Merseyside's big two have had some classy defenders through the years, men like Alan Hansen and Ray Wilson have given new dimensions to the art of defending. Few, however, have come close to the amazing Warnford Cresswell (he should have received an award for playing football with a name like that). The great Charlie Buchan said, recalling seeing Warney play the French virtually on his own while playing for England in Paris:

"Warney did not believe in running. I don't think he ever sprinted during the whole of his 18 year career, but he was rarely caught out of position. He looked a move ahead, and with his shuffling stiff-legged canter, took up the best position to check the opposition. Warney seldom tackled an opponent when he had possession of the ball. He stood beside him — at times moved along with him — until he practically forced him to part with the ball. Whatever happened Warney was not really beaten, he was usually between the opposing forwards and the goal."

Cresswell represented England many times as a schoolboy, including one match, in 1915, when he played centre half against Wales at Birkenhead Park. He joined Everton, from

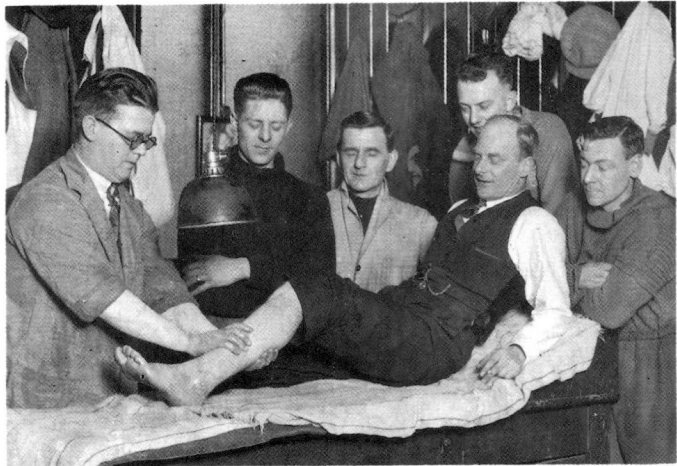

Everton masseur and Geoffrey Howe lookalike 'Gentleman' Barker works on Warney Cresswell as Ted Sagar, Harry Cooke, Tom White and Arthur Rigby look on.

Sunderland, in 1927 and during his nine years with the Blues won every honour in the game. As a 13-year-old he figured in one of the smallest transfers of all time, when he changed boys' clubs in his native South Shields for the princely sum of 2s 6d.

PLAY UP AND PLAY THE GAME

Surprising as it may seem Eton and Harrow have played a significant part in Merseyside's footballing history. Liverpool's oldest amateur club, Liverpool Ramblers, owes its existence to a couple of games played between sides of public schoolboys who were home for the Christmas holidays of 1881-1882. So successful were these matches that the following February a meeting was held in the Offices of James Bateson Sons and Co., a stockbrokers in Old Hall Street. As a result of the meeting it was decided to form an old public schoolboys football club. The club was to be called Liverpool Ramblers A.F.C.

The new club joined the Liverpool County F.A. and it should be noted that the only other of the then member clubs still in existence is Everton.

The colours they selected are still worn today — the orange and blue of one of Eton's most famous footballing houses, well known at the time for its war-cry:

And Eton may play with a pill if they please.
And Harrow may stick to their Cheshire Cheese.
And Rugby their overgrown egg; but here
Is the game of the perfect sphere.

The Ramblers' first fixture list in season 1882-1883 included teams such as Bootle, Southport, Nottingham, St. Mary's (Kirkdale), Blackburn Rovers, Wirral, Cambridge Wanderers and Burscough.

The Ramblers' first home was behind the Aigburth Hotel, but having no changing rooms they were forced to rely on the generosity of Liverpool Cricket Club and use of their pavilion. Before moving to their present home in Moor Lane, Crosby, in 1934, they used a pitch off Smithdown Road and for two seasons the ground at Liverpool Cricket Club, followed by a number of pitches in the Crosby area.

The club has the distinction of being the first English club to play a game in Dublin. The match was on 16th December, 1887, when Dublin University formed the opposition. The luck of the Irish favoured the home side who ran out 6-4 winners.

A few years later the Ramblers joined forces with Blackburn Etrurians to send a side called the English Pilgrims to play in a tournament for the King of the Belgians Cup in Brussels. Despite the after-effects of a particularly stormy crossing and the generous night-time hospitality of their hosts, the Pilgrims won their way through to the final, only to lose 6-5 by a penalty in the last minute of extra time.

Many well-known professionals have helped with the Ramblers' coaching over the years, Hunter Hart, Jock Thomson, Alex Steven, Maurice Lindley, Harry Potts, Peter Farrell and Johnny Wheeler often assisted by Ronnie Moran.

The spirit of the club is truly amateur, and since their formation they have never taken part in any form of league competition, although they have entered a number of cup competitions.

The essence of the Ramblers may best be seen in the story of Tommy Lashmar who was the reluctant star of a bizarre transfer deal. In 1924 the Corinthians, prior to their 1939 amalgamation with the Casuals, came to Liverpool en-route for a tour of the U.S.A.

Their recognised goalkeeper had been unable to travel with them and was to follow-on later in the tour. Prior to embarking from the Landing Stage the Ramblers treated their guests to lunch, which in the great tradition of Liverpool lunches ended some considerable time after closing time.

Players and officials from both clubs stood at the foot of the gangway discussing prospects for the tour and much sympathy was expressed for the Corinthians having to leave without their goalkeeper. Suddenly just as the gang-plank was about to be raised Lashmar, a dab hand between the sticks, found himself unceremoniously bundled aboard. He was wearing suit and hat, but as a last minute gesture to Atlantic weather his mackintosh was thrown aboard as the liner pulled away. Lashmar's 'fond' farewells were lost in the howl of the ship's siren and the screech of the gulls.

As an after-thought a change of clothes and his boots were sent on later. Liverpool Ramblers, truly gentlemen and players.

BESSIE AT PLAY

Bessie Braddock was not only a hard working MP on behalf of her constituents but always took time to be involved in the lighter side of life. She was a regular at the Stadium and a life long devotee of Everton F.C. Here she is seen in Liverpool during the filming of 'Violent Playground'.

Bessie again, this time with Liverpool's Dairy Princess Patricia McHugh and Britain's drink more milk girl Zoe Newton (remember her?) in Liverpool in 1959. Bessie commented "I've always drunk milk. I am a well-known figure in the House of Commons for drinking milk, when other people are drinking things which are not quite so good for them". Professor Andrew Semple Liverpool's Medical Officer of Health mentioned that the City's schools were the first in the country to provide both pasteurised and tuberculin tested milk for their pupils.

The 1950 team about to set off from Kent on the Cross Channel Row.

MESSING ABOUT ON THE RIVER

Any brave soul who ventured down by the Mersey during the great gale of 1913 would have witnessed the death throes of one of the strangest vessels (if you could call it that) ever seen on the Mersey. It was the floating clubhouse of the Mersey Rowing Club. The boathouse was launched in 1840 along with the club, which for many years was pre-eminent among the rowing clubs of the North West.

Club members performed with distinction at the major events on the rowing calendar, the Head of the River races on the Thames and the Dee, and of course Henley.

One of their Henley trips before the First World War was less than a great success. The team, either psyched up by the trainer or still suffering from the previous night's excesses,

The floating boathouse, headquarters of the Mersey Rowing Club from 1840 until it was wrecked during the great gale of 1913.

started down the course in fine style only to be informed from the bank that the race had been cancelled and they were racing against themselves. Unfortunately by this time their boat had begun to take on water and was in danger of sinking, even worse all their clothes and more importantly their brandy had been taken by the trainer to the finishing line. There was no alternative but to make a dash for the line, alternately bailing and rowing. Gallant gentlemen all, they went down with the ship within a snifter's length of the brandy.

The club struggled for members as time went by, at one annual general meeting the 'recruiting sergeant' reported; "of late years, young men do not care for the hard work of rowing, I wish I could rid them of the fatal liking of golf and other tame rabbit games, which are only fit for old fogeys like me". The Mersey Rowing Club finally sank beneath the waves in 1957 but has been re-floated in the re-developed South Docks.

While the Mersey Rowing Club has had a chequered career another club has kept the flag flying for Mersey oarsmen through the years. The Liverpool Victoria Rowing Club based at Birkenhead's West Float celebrated its centenary in 1984.

The West Float in December is a venue to dispel the image of rowing as sport for yahooing upper class twits in striped blazers and champagne stained flannels, but December sees one of the clubs most popular events. The annual Head of the Float race started life as a pre-Christmas 'jolly' for the members but before long crews from other clubs wanted to take part and the event began to take shape. Now over 40 crews, many of them women, regularly compete in conditions that would sometimes make a polar bear jump back on top of his glacier mint.

KOP THIS

Nine-year-old Liverpool fan Christopher Challinor probably has the strangest club momento of all. Christopher needed a dental plate fitting and although his dentist likes to arrange to make the plates in the children's favourite colours, the technicians exceeded themselves with Christopher's. Only one problem however — his mother explained that Christopher spends more time with it out of his mouth showing it to his friends!

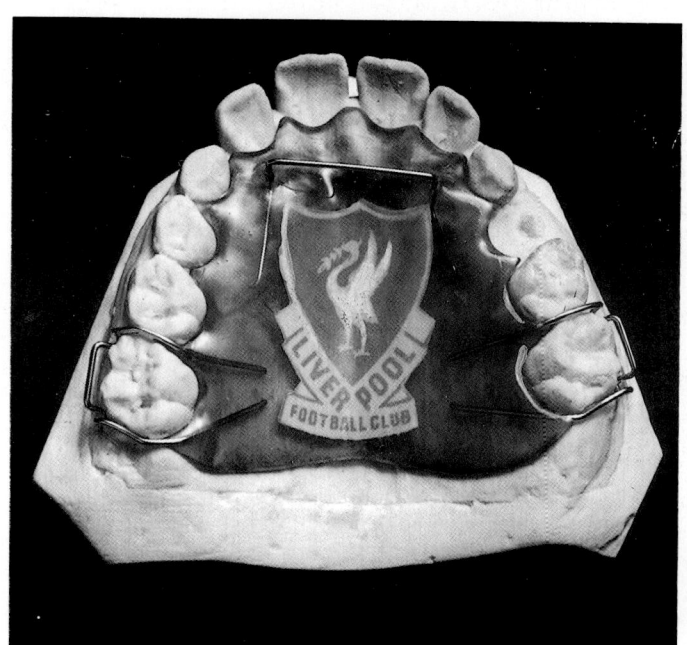

Oh I say it's Don Maskell putting some potential Lottie Dods or Angela Buxtons through their paces at West Kirby in 1952. That's Fred Perry looking on.

Giant Ludo aboard a Mersey Sea Fort in 1944.

L. Dickinson of the Lancashire Walking Club won the All England 10 Miles Walk in Liverpool in 1932.

*Despite a fall near the finish which damaged his cycle and carrying **that** number Liverpool's Stan Brittain pushes his bike across the line to win the Swedish Six Day Cycle Race in Stockholm in September 1957.*

ACT NATURALLY

In 1987 Eric Hardy made the record books, the Guinness Book of Records to be exact, for being the longest regular contributor to a newspaper, he was then in his 60th year as natural history correspondent of the Daily Post. That short statement does little justice to a man who is quite simply the best in his field.

Eric Hardy's interest in nature was awakened when he went to visit his uncle, a naturalist, in the Midlands. His mind was quickly made up, he wanted to be a naturalist, and he decided to finance his love affair with nature by earning money as a freelance journalist. His headmaster at Liverpool's Holt High School, where Eric was opening bat in the cricket team, saw little future for him, and suggested he might get a job as a park-keeper in Sefton Park.

Undismayed by his headmaster's attitude he armed himself with a second hand typewriter, bought for 30 shillings in Smithdown Road and started work. Over fifty years later he still works with the same restless energy he started out with as a boy. Over the years he has written thousands of articles, made hundreds of broadcasts, as well as finding time to write books and to lecture.

He founded the Merseyside Naturalists Association in 1939 and made his first broadcast in 1936. He was very concious of the traditional class barriers that seem to separate nature lovers into certain classes:

"Whether you are a duke or a docker you have the same right to know and study,

Eric Hardy.

"There has been the idea that privileged people alone should be told what's going on, the group who perhaps used to be regarded as the doctors, retired clergy, and school mistress nature set. But there is no ownership of wild birds or plants, although some would try to do that."

His ambition for the future is to find out more about prehistoric man in Liverpool. But as for his present ambition:

"I want to be the link between the Merseyside countryside and the Merseyside resident."

In that aim he has been an unqualified success.

BIG STRONG BOY

Six-feet two and 14½ stone sounds more like a Rugby League star. It certainly doesn't seem to describe one of the greatest swimmers Britain has ever known.

Yet that was the towering muscular physique of a young man at Wallasey Grammar School who mixed exams and swimming endeavour to challenge the world.

Neil McKechnie will, no doubt be remembered for holding simultaneously every English free-style record from 100 yards to a mile. He also held several British records at the same time.

He never managed to achieve a European or world best time but he could well have robbed himself of this when he retired somewhat prematurely from competitive swimming.

His meteoric rise to fame saw him make numerous television appearances and broadcasts, and he was television's Sportsboy of the Year in 1955.

It was that year, that was perhaps his most successful. He held 16 national records including the five from 100 yards to a mile — the 100, 220, 440, 880 yards and mile.

He was the very first swimmer for half a century to hold them simultaneously but to put him ahead of the field he also held the 110 yards backstroke record.

McKechnie was honoured by Wallasey Corporation when they granted him the freedom of the town's swimming baths.

Local representatives in the 1956 Olympics were guests of honour at a pre-Olympics dance in Liverpool hosted by the International Sports Fellowship. Branch chairman Austin Rawlinson shakes hands with Anne Morton (swimming) watched by left to right (back) Harry Sharratt (football), Haydn Rigby (swimming), George Bromilow (football), Neil McKechnie, left to right (front), John Geddes and Stan Brittan (cycling) and Tony Hollis and Joyce Coates who competed in the winter Olympics.

Bernie Start.

CAFE SOCIETY

If Mathew Street was the scene of the scene during the sixties, then, for more affluent scousers and arty types, Hardman Street was the the scene of the seventies. While Eric's held sway with the punks and real music enthusiasts down at the sharp end of town, up on the hill things were stirring. The area had always had an 'arty' feel and the pubs like the Phil, the Nook, the Cracke, and Peter Kavanagh's helped generate the Greenwich Village atmosphere.

Into this fertile soil, came new wine bars such as Streets, cosmopolitan restaurants, where you were afraid of looking ignorant so you didn't ask what it was you were eating, and most important of all, Kirklands.

Kirklands was the brainchild of Bernie Start, an ex-Liverpool Institute lad from Everton. He got the idea for Kirklands after visiting a wine bar in Southport. The building had started life as a homeopathic dispensary, subsequently becoming a church, and then a bakery owned by Kirkland Brothers who were bakers to Queen Victoria. The formula, with the cafe-bar downstairs and the music and events upstairs was an instant winner. With the old O'Connor's Tavern (now renamed Chaucer's) across the road, and the Phil at the top of the hill, the street and its environs filled in with eateries to satisfy all tastes, and clubs to pose in, to your heart's content.

If Hardman Street was the home of Cafe Society in the seventies, then Deaf School provided the backing music. Deaf School had its origins in the Liverpool College of Art in Hope Street, and took their name from the fact that they used to practice in the old Liverpool school for the Deaf.

Between 1974 and 1978, when they split up, they had an impact over and above their record sales and number of appearances. They never had a record in the singles chart, although their albums sold well. Their success was in influencing other musicians and singers, and pointing the direction out of that dreadful Sargasso Sea, that was the pop music of the mid-seventies.

In 1975 they entered the Melody Maker rock band of the year contest, for a laugh, and won. That put them on the national map. For the Liverpool music fan of the seventies the names of Enrico Cadillac Jnr., Eric Shark, Bette Bright, Clive Langer, Frankie Average, the Rev. Max Ripple, Tim Whittaker and Ian Ritchie, slip off the tongue as easy as those of John, Paul, George and the other one, did a decade earlier.

One reason they never made it big was possibly the fact that they were so difficult to categorise. After their tremendously successful reunion concert in June 1988 in their old stamping ground of Hardman Street, one critic wrote:

"They manage to combine sophisticated, cleverly constructed music with a rush of energy to equal any of the punk bands who came after them. With hindsight they have a body of quite remarkable songs, pulling styles as diverse as soul and sleaze, glam and raucous rock into a varied but characteristic style and painting pictures of stylised street level glamour which the audience can relate to."

Great music, shame about the critic.

NEW KID IN TOWN

Hogan 'Kid' Bassey from the village of Urck Ubet in Greek Town, Calabar in East Nigeria, became one of Merseyside's sporting heroes of the fifties. He arrived in Liverpool three days before Christmas 1951, won his first Stadium fight against Ray Hillyard from Leeds in four rounds, and went on to capture the heart of fight fans both here and in his homeland, where he was a national hero.

He won the world featherweight championship in 1957, the first Nigerian to achieve world honours, and was awarded the M.B.E. in 1958.

April 1958 and the 'Kid' returns home after his successful defence against Richard Moreno in Los Angeles.

Hogan says goodbye to Liverpool manager Phil Taylor in August 1958 before leaving for the States for six months. Bassey was a keen Reds fan and arranged for match reports to be sent to him while he was away. That's a very youthful looking Ronnie Moran on the right.

Bassey has lost to Davey Moore in America but to the residents of Carter Street he's still their champ. August 1959.

Hogan 'Kid' Bassey as World champion 'Kicks off' to start a ladies football match between Corinthians and Nomads at Stanley Greyhound Track.

FIRST RACE

The first authenticated race meeting was held at Chester in 1540. Subsequently, the Chester Cup became probably the first handicap to be won by a murderer — Palmer the Poisoner, in 1853. He won about £14,000, but lost most of it a few weeks later by laying his winnings against the horse West Australian in the Derby. "Have you nothing to regret, William?" asked his clergyman brother when, after killing numerous friends and relations, Palmer arrived at the scaffold. "Yes," said the poisoner, "I have never ceased to reproach myself for betting against West Australian."

GET ME TO THE RACE ON TIME

The Worlds leading authority on the Grand National has to be from Liverpool. And he is. Bubbling and diminutive, Reg Green was born in Everton and he and his family were bombed out of their home in Great Homer Street during the dark days of the Second World War. A Wartime visit to Aintree with his father when the course was host to thousands of American Military Personnel, fired his imagination as his father related stories of the geat Nationals of the 1920's and 30's.

Reg was determined to see the race and his dream came true in 1964 when Lovely Cottage won the first post war race. Since then Reg has missed only one National, but despite his incredible knowledge he had to wait until 1987 for his first winner (Maori Venture at 28-1).

Reg's love of the National knows no bounds.

In 1960 he found out, to his horror, that his wedding day coincided with the National. Not only that, but the timing was such that he couldn't get to Aintree to see the race at all. Reg pleaded with an unsympathetic Rev. Nicolls at Everton's St. George's Church to bring the time forward. The Vicar eventually relented and fitted Reg in at an earlier time. The service over, Reg and new wife, Brenda, made a brief appearance at the reception at Sampson and Barlow's in London Road before jumping in a taxi for the dash to Aintree. No handicap or hurdle proves too great for Reg, he and Brenda were in time for the race.

Reg is the author of the definitive book on the National, 'A Race Apart' published in 1988.

As Reg is a noted Scouseologist the following Aintree tit bits were quadruple checked for their accuracy (Don't ring us Reg).

The Grand National Steeplechase course is 4 miles 856 yards long. There are 30 fences, all the fences are jumped twice, except number 15, the Chair, and number 16, the Water. Becher's Brook is named after Captain Becher who, during the 1839 Grand Liverpool Steeplechase, was thrown from his mount, Conrad, and landed in the brook that now bears his name.

Jenny Pitman made history in 1983 when she became the first woman to train a National winner, as Corbiere held off a late challenge from Greasepaint to win. Ten years earlier her husband, Richard Pitman, was involved in a similar dramatic finish, when his mount, Crisp, was caught on the run-in, and pipped at the post by Red Rum.

The ladies stole the headlines the previous year, in 1982, when Geraldine Rees became the first woman to complete the National course, on Cheers. The race that year was won by Grittar, ridden by Dick Saunders, at forty-eight years of age, the oldest man ever to win the race.

In 1961 Nicolaus Silver became only the second grey to win the race, the first being The Lamb 1868 and 1871. 1961 was also notable for the appearance of the Russians at Aintree in an early attempt at 'Glasnot', sadly for East-West relations the three horses, Epigraf II, Grifel and Reljef, failed to complete the course, in fact Epigraf was even withdrawn before the race. The next visit from behind the Iron Curtain was not until 1986, when Essex from Czechoslovakia, became the first entry from that country since Gyi Lovam in 1931. Essex fared no better than the Russians.

Appropriately, the first — and probably the last — man to jump the Grand National course without a horse was a Merseysider: Tom Scott. It was in 1870 that Scott, a noted athlete, one of whose sons became Mayor of Bootle, jumped the course. The only concession that was allowed to him was that he was permitted to take the water jump in the reverse direction.

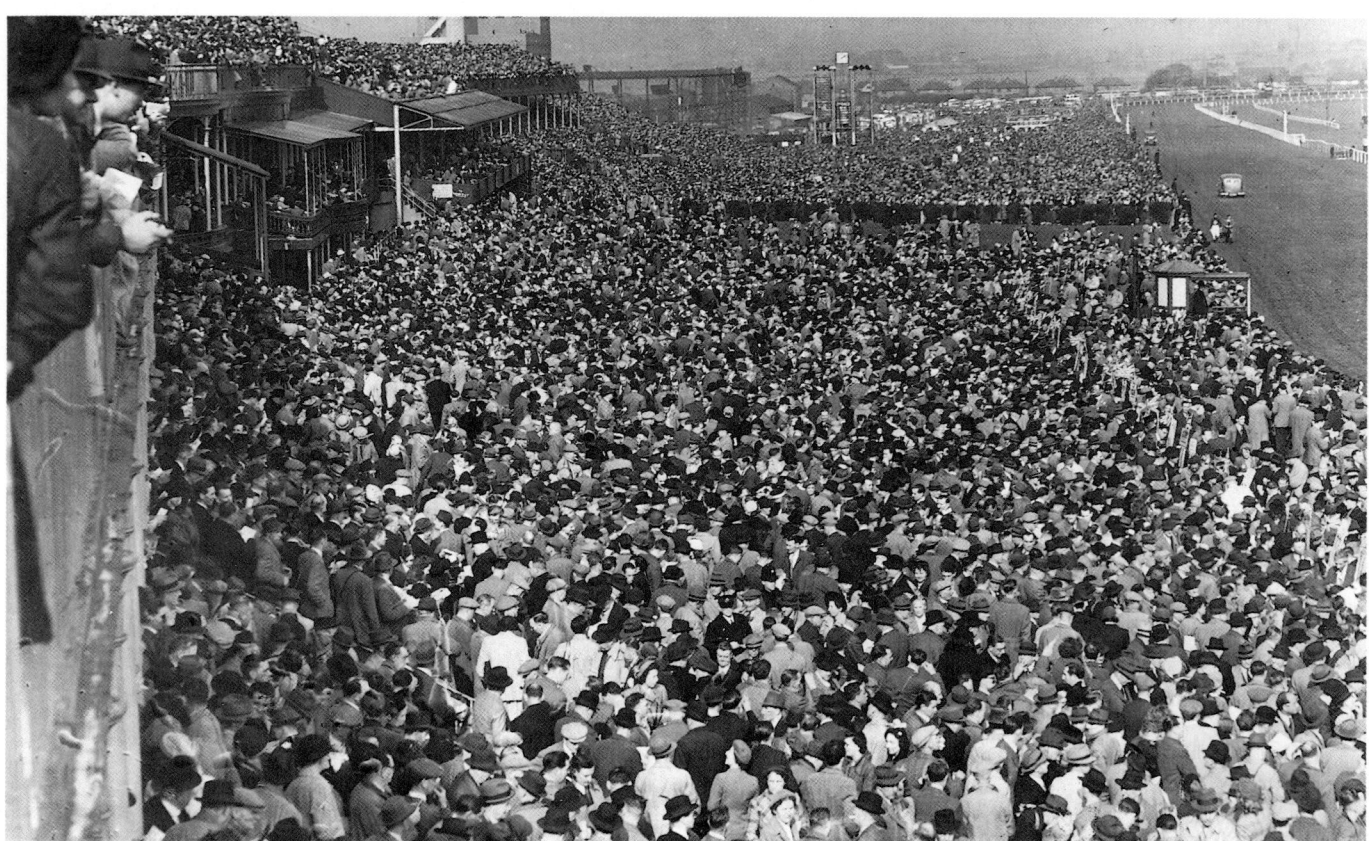

Part of the crowd in 1950.

THE AINTREE IRON

The 'Iron Lady' of Aintree passed away peacefully in her sleep in June 1980. Mirabel Topham died in Paddock Lodge, in the grounds of her beloved Aintree racecourse. The former actress and ex-Gaiety girl finally left the stage where she had starred for 40 years, she was 88.

Right to the end, although she was too ill to attend the National, the family links with Aintree were maintained by the sponsorship of the Topham Trophy.

Mrs. Topham's first taste of the limelight came when, as an eight-year-old, she took to the stage like her father and younger sister before her. Her career brought her to Liverpool, where she met her husband Arthur Ronald Topham.

In 1922 she saw her first Grand National, ironically a horse called Music Hall was the winner.

In 1935 she became a director of the Topham family business at Aintree, and began her amazing association with the great race.

Her colourful career was off to a flying start, when, within two years she was involved in a legal battle over the dismissal of her Clerk of the Course. She took on the BBC, refusing to let them broadcast the Grand National, and organising her own commentary.

She demanded a square deal for racecourses, battling with the racing news agencies and raising the rental of on-course telephones.

She eventually signed a deal in 1960 to televise the race, but the crowds began to dwindle and the huge upkeep of Aintree became too much to bear. In 1964 at the age of 72 Mrs. Topham said, the course she had bought from Lord Sefton in 1949 for £275,000, was to be sold for commercial development. The 1965 National would be the last. The on-off saga of Aintree continued for nine years until 1973, when a £3 million deal saw the course pass into the hands of Liverpool businessman Bill Davies.

Mriabel Topham once told a journalist that her ambition was to reach 80. When she passed that milestone, he asked her again what her aim was, "To reach ninety," she replied.

Unfortunately that was one hurdle this remarkable lady could not clear.

Jenny Pitman.

The original Mrs. T.

*The Royal Family watch Dick Francis mounting the Queen Mother's ill-fated
Devon Loch in 1954.*

Ginger McCain trainer of the great Red Rum.

*Hello, Hello, Hello — what's this in the corner then.
Checking the padlocks on
the stables.*

Gamekeeper James Mercer,
dog Lassie and Joey the ferret clearing the course.

We bet that Reg Green can guess what year.

The greatest.

Rummy wins in 1974 to the delight
of head lad Jackie Granger.

The Winners

Date	Winner	Jockey	Starters	Time
1839	LOTTERY	JEM MASON	17	14 mins 53 secs
1840	JERRY	MR. BRETHERTON	12	12 mins 30 secs
1841	CHARITY	MR. POWELL	11	13 mins 25 secs
1842	GAY LAD	TOM OLLIVER	15	13 mins 30 secs
1843	VANGUARD	TOM OLLIVER	16	Not taken
1844	DISCOUNT	MR. CRICKMERE	15	Just under 14 mins
1845	CURE-ALL	MR. W.J. LOFT	15	10 mins 47 secs
1946	PIONEER	W. TAYLOR	22	10 mins 46 secs
1847	MATTHEW	D. WYNNE	26	10 mins 39 secs
1848	CHANDLER	CAPT. J. L. LITTLE	29	11 mins 21 secs
1849	PETER SIMPLE	T. CUNNINGHAM	24	10 mins 56 secs
1850	ABD-EL-KADER	G.GREEN	32	9 mins 57½ secs
1851	ABD-EL-KADER	T. ABBOT	21	9 mins 59 secs
1852	MISS MOWBRAY	MR. A. GOODMAN	24	9 mins 58½ secs
1853	PETER SIMPLE	T. OLLIVER	21	10 mins 37½ secs
1854	BOURTON	J. TASKER	20	9 mins 59 secs
1855	WANDERER	J. HANLON	20	10 mins 25 secs
1856	FREETRADER	G. STEVENS	21	10 mins 9½ secs
1857	EMIGRANT	C. BOYCE	28	10 mins 6 secs
1858	LITTLE CHARLEY	W. ARCHER	16	11 mins 5 secs
1859	HALF CASTE	C. GREEN	20	10 mins 2 secs
1960	ANATIS	MR. THOMAS	19	Not taken
1861	JEALOUSY	J. KENDALL	24	10 mins 14 secs
1862	HUNTSMAN	H. LAMPLUGH	13	9 mins 30 secs
1863	EMBLEM	G. STEVENS	16	11 mins 20 secs
1864	EMBLEMATIC	G. STEVENS	25	11 mins 50 secs
1865	ALCIBIADE	CAPT. H. COVENTRY	23	11 mins 16 secs
1866	SALAMANDER	MR. A. GOODMAN	30	11 mins 5 secs
1867	GORTOLVIN	J. PAGE	23	10 mins 42 secs
1868	THE LAMB	MR. EDWARDS	21	Not taken
1869	THE COLONEL	G. STEVENS	22	11 mins
1870	THE COLONEL	G. STEVENS	23	10 mins 10 secs
1871	THE LAMB	MR. THOMAS	25	9 mins 35¾ secs
1872	CASSE TETE	J. PAGE	25	10 mins 14½ secs
1873	DISTURBANCE	MR. J. RICHARDSON	28	Watch stopped
1874	REUGNY	MR. J. RICHARDSON	22	10 mins 4 secs
1875	PATHFINDER	MR. THOMAS	19	10 mins 22 secs
1876	REGAL	J. CANNON	19	11 mins 14 secs
1877	AUSTERLITZ	MR. F. G. HOBSON	16	10 mins 10 secs
1878	SHIFNAL	J. JONES	12	10 mins 23 secs
1879	THE LIBERATOR	MR. G. MOORE	18	10 mins 12 secs
1880	EMPRESS	MR. T. BEASLEY	14	10 mins 20 secs
1881	WOODBROOK	MR. T. BEASLEY	13	11 mins 50 secs
1882	SEAMAN	LORD MANNERS	12	10 mins 42²/₅ secs
1883	ZOEDONE	COUNT C. KINSKY	10	11 mins 39 secs
1884	VOLUPTUARY	MR. E. P. WILSON	15	10 mins 5 secs
1885	ROQUEFORT	MR. E. P. WILSON	19	10 mins 10 secs
1886	OLD JOE	T. SKELTON	23	10 mins 14³/₅ secs
1887	GAMECOCK	W. DANIELS	16	10 mins 10¹/₅ secs
1888	PLAYFAIR	G. MAWSON	20	10 mins 12 secs
1889	FRIGATE	MR. T. BEASLEY	20	10 mins 1¹/₅ secs
1890	ILEX	A. NIGHTINGALL	16	10 mins 41⁴/₅ secs
1891	COME AWAY	MR. H. BEASLEY	21	9 mins 58 secs
1892	FATHER O'FLYNN	CAPT. E. R. OWEN	25	9 mins 48¹/₅ secs
1893	CLOISTER	W. DOLLERY	15	9 mins 32²/₅ secs
1894	WHY NOT	A. NIGHTINGALL	14	9 mins 45²/₅ secs
1895	WILD MAN FROM BORNEO	MR. JOSEPH WIDGER	19	10 mins 32 secs
1896	THE SOARER	MR. D. G. M. CAMPBELL	28	10 mins 11¹/₅ secs
1897	MANIFESTO	T. KAVANAGH	28	9 mins 49 secs
1898	DROGHEDA	J. GOURLEY	25	9 mins 43³/₅ secs
1899	MANIFESTO	G. WILLIAMSON	19	9 mins 49⁴/₅ secs
1900	AMBUSH II	A. ANTHONY	16	10 mins 1²/₅ secs
1901	GRUDON	A. NIGHTINGALL	24	9 mins 47⁴/₅ secs
1902	SHANNON LASS	D. READ	21	10 mins 3³/₅ secs
1903	DRUMCREE	P. WOODLAND	23	10 mins 9²/₅ secs
1904	MOIFAA	A. BIRCH	26	9 mins 58³/₅ secs
1905	KIRKLAND	F. MASON	27	9 mins 48⁴/₅ secs
1906	ASCETIC'S SILVER	MR. A. HASTINGS	23	9 mins 34²/₅ secs
1907	EREMON	A. NEWEY	23	9 mins 47½ secs
1908	RUBIO	H. B. BLESTSOE	24	10 mins 33¹/₅ secs
1909	LUTTEUR III	G. PARFREMENT	32	9 mins 53⁴/₅ secs
1910	JENKINSTOWN	R. CHADWICK	25	10 mins 44¹/₅ secs
1911	GLENSIDE	MR. J. R. ANTHONY	26	10 mins 35 secs
1912	JERRY M.	E. PIGGOTT	24	10 mins 13²/₅ secs
1913	COVERTCOAT	P. WOODLAND	22	10 mins 19 secs
1914	SUNLOCH	W. J. SMITH	20	9 mins 58⁴/₅ secs
1915	ALLY SLOPER	MR. J. R. ANTHONY	20	9 mins 47⁴/₅ secs
		THE WAR YEARS 1916, 1917, 1918		
1919	POETHLYN	E. PIGGOTT	22	10 mins 8²/₅ secs
1920	TROYTOWN	MR. J. R. ANTHONY	24	10 mins 20²/₅ secs
1921	SHAUN SPADAH	F. B. REES	35	10 mins 26 secs
1922	MUSIC HALL	L. B. REES	32	9 mins 55⁴/₅ secs
1923	SERGEANT MURPHY	CAPT. G. H. BENNET	28	9 mins 36 secs
1924	MASTER ROBERT	R. TRUDGILL	30	9 mins 40 secs
1925	DOUBLE CHANCE	MAJOR J. P. WILSON	33	9 mins 42⁴/₅ secs
1926	JACK HORNER	W. WATKINSON	30	9 mins 36 secs
1927	SPRIG	T. E. LEADER	37	10 mins 20¹/₅ secs
1928	TIPPERARY TIM	MR. W. DUTTON	42	10 mins 23²/₅ secs
1929	GREGALACH	R. EVERETT	66	9 mins 47²/₅ secs
1930	SHAUN GOILIN	T. B. CULLINAN	41	9 mins 40³/₅ secs
1931	GRAKLE	R. LYAL	43	9 mins 32⁴/₅ secs
1932	FORBRA	J. HAMXEY	36	9 mins 44³/₅ secs
1933	KELLSBORO' JACK	D. WILLIAMS	34	9 mins 28 secs
1934	GOLDEN MILLER	G. WILSON	30	9 mins 20²/₅ secs
1935	REYNOLDSTOWN	MR. F. FURLONG	27	9 mins 20¹/₅ secs
1936	REYNOLDSTOWN	MR. F. WALWYN	35	9 mins 37⁴/₅ secs
1937	ROYAL MAIL	E. WILLIAMS	33	9 mins 59⁴/₅ secs
1938	BATTLESHIP	B. HOBBS	36	9 mins 27 secs
1939	WORKMAN	T. HYDE	37	9 mins 42¹/₅ secs
1940	BOGSKAR	M. A. JONES	30	9 mins 20³/₅ secs
1946	LOVELY COTTAGE	CAPT. R. PETRE	34	9 mins 38¹/₅ secs
1947	CAUGHOO	E. DEMPSEY	57	10 mins 3⁴/₅ secs
1948	SHEILA'S COTTAGE	A. P. THOMPSON	43	9 mins 25²/₅ secs
1949	RUSSIAN HERO	L. McMORROW	43	9 mins 24¹/₅ secs
1950	FREEBOOTER	J. POWER	49	9 mins 24¹/₅ secs
1951	NICKEL COIN	J. A. BULLOCK	36	9 mins 48⁴/₅ secs
1952	TEAL	A. P. THOMPSON	47	9 mins 21½ secs
1953	EARLY MIST	B. MARSHALL	31	9 mins 22⅘ secs
1954	ROYAL TAN	B. MARSHALL	29	9 mins 32⅘ secs
1955	QUARE TIMES	P. TAFFE	30	10 mins 19¹/₅ secs
1956	E.S.B.	D. V. DICK	29	9 mins 21²/₅ secs
1957	SUNDEW	F. T. WINTER	35	9 mins 42²/₅ secs
1958	MR. WHAT	A. FREEMAN	31	9 mins 59⁴/₅ secs
1959	OXO	M. SCUDAMORE	34	9 mins 37⁴/₅ secs
1960	MERRYMAN II	G. SCOTT	26	9 mins 26¹/₅ secs
1961	NICKOLAUS SILVER	H. R. BEASLEY	35	9 mins 22³/₅ secs
1962	KILMORE	F. T. WINTER	32	9 mins 50 secs
1963	AYALA	P. BUCKLEY	47	9 mins 35⁴/₅ secs
1964	TEAM SPIRIT	G. W. ROBINSON	33	9 mins 46⁴/₅ secs
1965	JAY TRUMP	MR. T. G. SMITH	47	9 mins 30³/₅ secs
1966	ANGLO	T. NORMAN	47	9 mins 52⁴/₅ secs
1967	FOINAVON	J. BUCKINGHAM	44	9 mins 49³/₅ secs
1968	RED ALLIGATOR	B. FLETCHER	45	9 mins 28⁴/₅ secs
1969	HIGHLAND WEDDING	E. P. HARTY	30	9 mins 30⁴/₅ secs
1970	GAY TRIP	P. TAFFE	28	9 mins 38 secs
1971	SPECIFY	J. COOK	38	9 mins 34¹/₅ secs
1972	WELL TO DO	G. THORNER	42	10 mins 8²/₅ secs
1973	RED RUM	B. FLETCHER	38	9 mins 1.9 secs
1974	RED RUM	B. FLETCHER	42	9 mins 20.3 secs
1975	L'ESCARGOT	T. CARBERRY	31	9 mins 31.1
1976	RAG TRADE	J. BURKE	32	9 mins 20.9 secs
1977	RED RUM	T. STACK	42	9 mins 30.3 secs
1978	LUCIOUS	B. R. DAVIES	37	9 mins 33.9 secs
1979	RUBSTIC	M. BARNES	34	9 mins 52.9 secs
1980	BEN NEVIS	MR. G. FENWICK	30	10 mins 17.4 secs
1981	ALDANITI	R. CHAMPION	39	9 mins 47.2 secs
1982	GRITTAR	MR. C. SAUNDERS	39	9 mins 12.6 secs
1983	CORBIERE	B. DE HAAN	41	9 mins 47.4 secs
1984	HALLO DANDY	N. DOUGHTY	40	9 mins 21.4 secs
1985	LAST SUSPECT	H. DAVIES	40	9 mins 42.7 secs
1986	WEST TIP	R. DUNWOODY	40	9 mins 33 secs
1987	MAORI VENTURE	S. C. KNIGHT	40	9 mins 19.3 secs
1988	RHYME 'N' REASON	J. POWELL	40	9 mins 53.5 secs

THE STARS AT AINTREE

Gregory Peck and wife Veronique with Tom Dreaper trainer of Peck's horse Owen's Sedge in 1963.

Randolph Scott and his wife Marion. Marion's horse Battleship won in 1938, ridden by Bruce Hobbs the youngest jockey to win the race.

Emlyn Hughes with his 1979 National entry Wayward Scot.

Veteran jockey Tim Durant (right) gets some advice from Burgess Meredith, who plays the Penguin in the Batman series, on how to negotiate the fences. Together at a dinner at the Adelphi.

WACKER JACKO

Europe's biggest pop concert was held at Aintree Racecourse, Liverpool, on September 13th, 1988, starring superstar Michael Jackson. 125,000 people attended and apart from about 40 minor injuries in the crush, the organisers and the police voted it a major success.

BLACKIE

Passengers leaving James Street Station on an August morning in 1971 were astonished to be met by a young couple, who without explanation, thrust a small cardboard box into their hands, saying "Here's your lunch."

They were even more surprised when they opened up the boxes, and in each one found:—

One green coloured batch, with paste and beetroot filling.
One cake (green and blue stripes).
One sausage roll (turquoise pastry and green sausage).
One cocktail cigarette (pink with gold tip).

Inside the box was a small slip of paper with the words: "All the food in this carton is edible."

One week later the 99 bus between Penny Lane and Gillmoss was the scene of another bizarre happening; passengers were greeted, as they boarded the bus, by four young men and a girl, offering tea or coffee, a morning paper, and a cigarette (you could be arrested for that today).

Very odd you may think, but stranger still on that August Monday morning, as Christine Kilty from Wallasey left James Street Station she was confronted by a huge six-foot by four photograph, and she was sure she recognised the girl pictured walking along James Street. Closer examination proved her first impression to be correct, for the girl in the picture was Christine herself. Then she recalled seeing two girls and a young man taking photographs in James Street the previous week.

Another picture of a mystery girl in a leather coat, appeared at Exchange Station, and the staff of a cake shop in Tithebarn Street found a gigantic 'snap' of themselves when they turned up for work that morning.

Next in this strange sequence of events came dozens of portraits of pigeons adorning public buildings in the city. The culmination of these happenings was at Midnight on the 24th August when a gigantic ice sculpture as dumped outside the City Planning Office in the Strand. In a statement issued at noon the following day Mr. Anthony Moscadini the City Planning Officer said: "It's melting slowly, but otherwise little is happening to it . . . we don't know who's behind it, but we suspect it's the same people who went round putting faces and bow ties on parking meters."

Finally the culprit owned up, it was the Great George's Project, better known as the Blackie.

The Blackie was the brainchild of the husband and wife team of Bill and Wendy Harpe. Darlington-born Bill first came to Liverpool in 1961, he worked as a supply teacher for Liverpool City Council, appeared at the Empire in pantomime with Tommy Steele and Morecambe and Wise and choreographed ballet for the Bluecoat Bill left Liverpool in 1964 to direct the Cardiff Commonwealth Arts Festival (with his wife Wendy as Assistant Director), but returned to the city, and the public spotlight, when he was appointed as Artistic Director in charge of the opening celebrations for the Metropolitan Cathedral, Wendy took charge of the Bluecoat. Arts Forum. We knew we were in for some fun when she was asked, in connection with his choreographing of the Cathedral's opening mass, what was the best dance performance he had seen recently, he replied "the North Koreans at Goodison Park."

The Blackie started life as a Congregational Chapel on the edge of Liverpool's Chinatown, it was built in 1772 and closed in 1967. At the time of the church's closure the Harpe's were

Bill and Wendy Harpe.

Christine Kilty on film.

looking for a base for a community arts centre, and the building seemed to fit the bill. The couple didn't have the £7,000 purchase price, but help was at hand in the shape of Peter Moores, who found the necessary cash.

The Harpe's intention was to "change the building into a playground of the contemporary arts." In 1968, the Blackie opened with "The To-Hell-With-Human-Rights-Show," described as an extended theatre game with the audience providing the action, the tone for the next twenty years had been set. In spite of conflicting advice ranging from "you should be running a youth club," to, "it's impossible to run an arts centre which is not middle class," the Harpe's forged ahead and the Blackie established a name for itself as the prototype inner city community arts centre, which has been copied all over Britain.

In 1987 the smoke-stained exterior of the Blackie (which gave it its nickname) was cleaned up giving it a new image, but inside the arts' mix was as wide-ranging as ever; everything from painting to writing, video to theatre, and dance to poetry, all blended together with that vital ingredient, local involvement.

In May 1988 the Blackie celebrated its twentieth birthday with a programme which gives a good summary of the Blackie's range of activities, poetry, folk music, Chinese and Indian music, snooker, chess, kite making, and a children's party.

When the Blackie opened Bill Harpe said; "We have five years of hard work in front of us to achieve our aims." Two decades later the hard work still goes on to improve and expand Liverpool's unique "sports centre for the arts."

WOOLLY NUDES SHOCK HORROR

When four young Merseysiders, agreed to dress in crocheted costumes and take the part of living sculptures in avant garde arts performance, among shoppers in Liverpool's Church Street in 1980 they could never have dreamt they would end up behind bars.

The four, Hayley and Melani Fox, together with Mary Renouf and Nick Gaskin, dressed up in the costumes, designed by the Edinburgh artist, Alice Beberman, at the Open Eye Gallery in Whitechapel. The costumes known as 'Furbelows', were crocheted naked bodies. In Church Street a crowd of about sixty people gathered round as the 'Furbelows' went into their act. They had only just started, when the police intervened, arrested them, and later charged them with insulting behaviour likely to cause a breach of the peace. The four were found guilty and fined £25 each, much to the astonishment of the Open Eye Gallery and many others in the arts' world on Merseyside.

They appealed, but astonishingly the Judge, describing their costumes as "extravagant and obscene" and their behavious as "disgraceful and disgusting", replaced the fines with 14 days jail each.

This time there was no appeal. The four did their time, but the costumes were allowed to go free, maybe the police kept them under surveillance, thinking the crimes might follow a pattern.

THAT'S KEYNSHAM, SPELT K.E.Y.N.S.H.A.M. . . .

Everyone enjoys a flutter, and the centre of Britain's most popular regular 'investment' is right here on Merseyside. There were a number of football pools firms operating in Britain in the early 20's, but the real growth of the industry took place with two firms in Liverpool.

John Moores was working as a telegraphist for the Commercial Cable Company, when he got together with two other Cable Company employees in Liverpool to start a pools business. It was 1924, each drew £50 from the bank to start the venture, a small office was rented and 4,000 coupons were printed. Small boys were hired to distribute them at Manchester United's football ground. The takings for that first week in February 1924 were £4.7s.6d., and by the end of the season the three men had lost £600.

John Moores bought out his two partners for £200 each, but retained the name (one of the partners had been christened Colin Henry Littlewood).

With the help of a girl assistant and one of his sisters at weekends, John Moores persevered with Littlewoods Pools during the 1924-25 season, other members of the family came into the business and by 1928 he was handling about 50,000 coupons a week, with bets totalling over £4,500. The business was in profit, and the success story was under way.

Liverpool's other pools giant, Vernons, started in the city in September 1926, after Mr. Edmund Sangster had started the pools business in a small way in Preston. Edmund Sangster's son, Vernon, was the driving force behind the growth of the company, and as with Littlewoods, success came after a series of initial setbacks. Within a few years Vernons were in a position to build the first premises to be constructed specifically for football pools, in Aintree close to the racecourse.

Vernons continued to expand and diversify, and in November 1954 announced plans to build a three-wheeler car at their factory in Valley Road, Bidston. In today's 16 valve, hi-tech, turbo motor market the Gordon (yes, it really was called Gordon), wouldn't cut much ice. But don't rush to judgement, look at the description and specification. Arthur Johnson, the Liverpool Echo's motoring correspondent in the fifties, writes: "An attractive, sturdily built little vehicle, the Gordon is designed to catch the fancy of the married man with one or more small children, who is in the transitional stage of growing out of a motorcycle

---

THE FUN NEVER SETS ON MERSEYSIDE

It was a dull fight at the Stadium when someone at the back shouted.

"You may as well turn the bloody lights off".
Straight away a voice at the front replied.
"Leave 'em on — I'm readin'."

Harry was picking up his winnings at the betting shop, a 50-1 winner called Laurentic.

"What made you pick that one?" asked the bookie, counting the fivers reluctantly.

"I crossed on a ship called that," said Harry.

"Too bad you didn't cross on the Titanic," said the bookie.

combination, and being unable to afford a small car. The price in standard form is £269.17s.6d. (including purchase tax). A more expensive de-luxe vesion provides two outstanding driving mirrors, better quality hood and side screens, two colour body, and white-wall tyres, all for an extra £16.

"The power unit is a fan cooled Villiers 197cc two stroke, chain driving the offside rear wheel through a three speed gearbox, with reverse. Maximum speed is 45mph, and petrol consumption is 70mpg at a steady 30mph.

"The engine protrudes slightly from the bodyline on the offside, alongside the driver. It is partly cowled by a metal shield, and although it gets plenty of cooling air in this position, it hardly improves the car's looks. Also, because of the unusual position of the engine, the car has only one door — on the near side.

"A front bench seat has plenty of room for two hefty males, and behind the seat is a large luggage space capable of accommodating two children."

If any reader out there can tell us any more about this remarkable vehicle, or ever better, actually still owns one, we would love to hear from them. And if one is found who knows . . . Wally Scott could be persuaded to give up his Robin Reliant.

A pools winner in 1936 receives her cheque. She's obviously good at perms.

A Gordon for me? Well maybe not.

CARELESS HANDS

The morning of Saturday, December 9th, 1967 dawned clear but cold. Kopites listening to their radios were relieved to hear that, in spite of a covering of snow, the match at Anfield that afternoon was likely to be on. It was a crucial match for the Reds, as they were playing Leeds United and a good result would enable them to gain ground on the League leaders, Manchester United (Well it *was* over twenty years ago).

One way or another it was to turn out to be a rather musical weekend. In Southport's Lord Street, Mrs. Duncan Weldon, better known as pop singer Helen Shapiro, was settling into life as a housewife in her new flat. The following day tragedy was to strike, when a plane carrying the great soul singer, Otis Redding, crashed into the icy waters of Lake Wisconsin robbing the world of a unique talent.

At Anfield a 39,676 crowd saw the match get under way with the Reds in fine form. Skipper Ron Yeats was unwell, and Geoff Strong was having his first game in defence. The Hateley-Hunt combination up front was giving the 'Giraffe' and his co-defenders a rough time. It was no surprise when Hunt put Liverpool into a one goal lead with a sharp shot from close range. Just before half-time Leeds went two goals down with one of the strangest goals ever seen at Anfield. With the Leeds defence under no pressure Jack Charlton rolled a back-pass to his goalkeeper, Gary Sprake. Sprake fielded the ball and went to throw it out to his full-back, Terry Cooper. As the 'keeper drew his arm back the snowy ball shot from his grasp, and into the empty net behind him. This was the signal for one of the Kop's finest vocal performances, as one, they burst into a raucous version of Des O'Connor's 'Careless Hands'. Half-time brought no respite for the unfortunate Sprake, there are no prizes for guessing the first record on the turntable that day.

*A disconsolate Sprake after **that** goal. That's Jack Charlton looking on isn't it? Now what could he be saying? Our guess. "Never you mind Gary son, it could happen to anyone."*

To put the record straight because Sprake was an international goalie, here he turns a Thompson shot round the post and collects comfortably despite the attentions of Chris Lawler.

THE OPEN ROAD

Taking a hairpin on the Bwlch-Y-Groes pass during Liverpool Motor Clubs 24 hour trial in 1924.

One of the first motoring organisations in Britain (probably the first) was the Liverpool Self-Propelled Traffic Association who are known to have held trials for its members on Everton Brow, Liverpool in 1896. By 1902, this association had dissolved and as a result the Liverpool Motorcycle Club was formed in the same year, their first event being held on July 4th, 1903 in the form of a Speed Trial and Sprint on Southport Promenade which lasted throughout the day and evening. The name of the Club was formally changed in 1904 to The Liverpool Motor Club. By 1908, there were signs that interest in the club was declining and the organisation started to break up. However, an enthusiastic rider by the name of Frank Rees persuaded his friend Victor Horsman to help him contact all members, inviting them to a meeting, which resulted in the Club being re-formed as the Mersey Motor Club. This latter organisation prospered and their more popular events included the Pen-Y-Ball Hill Climb and the Colwyn Bay Speed Trials. Again, troubles hit the organisation in the form of differences of opinion with the committee, which led to break away clubs being formed — The Liverpool Autocycle Club and The Liverpool Amateur Motorcycle Club. The three organisations continued separate existences until just after the start of the First World War, when in 1915 Victor Horsman called a joint meeting of the three clubs and it was agreed that they should merge under the old title of the Liverpool Motor Club.

The Colwyn Bay Speed Trials continued to play an important role in the club's activities until 1928 when it became obvious that the increase in speed and resultant increase in braking distances might lead to the risk of riders crashing into a Pierrot Show held on the promenade.

Sir Alexander Jeans proprietor of the Liverpool Daily Post and Echo presented a solid Gold Cup to the Club in 1923 for a Reliability Trial. This particular award remains in existence to this day and is the only solid Gold Trophy in Motor Sport.

The first sand races were held on Wallasey beach in 1923 before a crowd of some 6,000 spectators. Races were also held in latter years on Formby and Southport beaches.

A unique part of the history of the Club occurred in January 1959 when the late Geoff Hunt who worked for Cunard, moved to New York and quickly established the New York Branch of the Liverpol Motor Club. This branch of the club grew rapidly and apart from running its own events, helped to promote in September 1960 the first of a series of International competitions held annually.

These comprised of a pre-arranged course, driving test, trial or sprint laid out on each side of the Atlantic and wherever possible both events were held on the same day when the times were recorded and phoned across. Whichever side recorded the best times kept the Trophy for a year.

WINTER SPORT

In the bitterly cold winter of 1987 Pat Royle from Eastham on Wirral raised a smile with a piece of driving which could have had disastrous consequences. Pat managed to drive 100 yards along the snow and ice covered Shropshire Union Canal at Broughton, Chester, thinking it was a road. Pat, an Inland Revenue rating officer, was on her way to inspect a local school when she made her near-fatal mistake.

"I drove along for about 100 yards thinking I was on a road. Suddenly, this man began shouting to me that I was in the middle of the canal.

"I reversed the car to where I had first joined what I took to be a road and it was then that I heard the ice crack. I was out of the car like a shot!"

Pat jumped to the safety of the towpath, but she almost lost her hired car when the ice broke as a breakdown wagon winched it clear. The car went under almost to roof level before being pulled out.

As Pat said later: "What a way to end 20 years' accident-free driving."

Skating at Calderstone park during that winter of 1963. Gillian McKnight of Huyton takes a break to warm her hands by a specially provided Corporation brazier.

It's 1952 and a determined skater travels past Banks Bridge near Burscough on the Leeds/Liverpool canal.

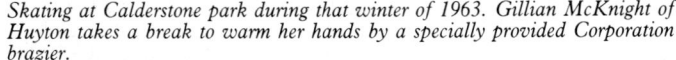

This is just not cricket.

Trying to avoid casualties, Birkenhead Corporation break up ice at Birkenhead Park.

An Echo photographer, trying to avoid the ice and snow which has gathered in his usual behind-the-goal position, takes this unusual shot of Jimmy Case centreing into the Blackburn goalmouth during an F.A. Cup tie in 1979. Terry McDermott seems to be in an offside position.

THE FUN NEVER SETS ON MERSEYSIDE

Mr. H. Smart, the Liverpool Licensee who has been mugged every week for the past three months on the way to the bank with the Pub takings, has announced his intention to quit.

"I've had enough," he said, "I can't take any more".

It is understood Mr. Smart leaves Liverpool next Tuesday with his family to start a new life in the Bahamas.

"What was Hitler's first name?"
"I know it, Billy, I don't need a clue".
"What was it then, Love?"
"Heil".

Billy Liddell and Kilkenny of Doncaster Rovers had clashed heads and were lying prone on the Anfield turf. With customary speed, six St. John ambulance men ran on with three stretchers.

Alan Arnell had not been playing well.

"Thank God for that," said the Kopite, "They're takin' Arnell off as well".

Tommy Smith couldn't understand Shankly's long face.

"What's up Boss — we won 5-0"?
"Aye, lad, but we lost the toss" said Bill.

THE FILM SET

So many films are shot in Liverpool these days that Bleasdale's description of the city 'being like a film set' seems true in more ways than one. It hasn't always been the case though. One of the earliest and most famous films to use Liverpool as its location was 'Waterfront' shot in the city in 1949. The film starred Richard Burton, no stranger to the city as he had had made his professional acting debut at the Royal Court in 1942, Robert Newton and Avis Scott. The film was based on the novel by Liverpool born John Brophy, the father of distinguished Irish writer Brigid Brophy.

Perhaps the most distinguished of contemporary Liverpool born film makers is award winning Terence Davies whose 1988 film 'Distant Voices, Still Lives' is an extraordinary recollection of Liverpool family life during wartime and after.

Avis Scott and Richard Burton (I wonder what Elizabeth would have thought of the mack) together with James McVey of Malcombe Place who played the Echo seller.

Mersey Film Teasers

1. The movies best Sherlock Holmes, he played him 14 times, was a member of a famous Liverpool family. Who was he and in what film did he play opposite Greta Garbo.

2. Can you remember where the following Liverpool cinemas were located. The Magnet, The Corona, The Cosy, Palace Kinematodrome.

3. Famous Liverpudlian, uncle of an Olympic medallist, who appeared in Carrington VC, The Missing Note, The Amorous Prawn, Joey Boy and The Spy With A Cold Nose, although he wasn't an actor.

4. His film debut was in Saraband for Dead Lovers, in 1948.

5. Wallasey born, he edited Sanders of the River, directed The Lavender Hill Mob, among many others.

John Walters of Carlingford Street and 18-year-old Sylvia Lashley of Crown Street, stand-ins for the film's two stars.

Local actor Hal Osmond a former Cammell Lairds rivet boy as he appeared in 'Waterfront' (yet another of those wonderful unclean period macks).

Frankie Vaughan looking anxious on the 'Cazzie' in a scene from "These Dangerous Years".

Technicians working on 'Ferry 'Cross the Mersey' set up a table in Victoria Street for an impromptu lunch break whilst filming in 1964.

The great Katherine Hepburn arrives at Liverpool docks after crossing from New York on Cunard's liner Media, in April 1951. She was in England to film 'The African Queen.'

Ringo with archetypal Sixties 'dolly bird' Patti Boyd in 'A Hard Day's Night'.

Camp life; somewhere between Rhyl and Prestatyn.

HAPPY DAYS IN HAPPILAND

Ah, the North Wales coast. That glittering sun kissed strip where all of us worth our salt had such magical times. In the days when we thought Benidorm was a tailor in North John Street, that Ibiza was something by Gilbert and Sullivan and going topless was leaving off your balaclava, we'd go there in droves. The bus into town, across on the ferry and the Crosville from Woodside to Prestatyn, Rhyl or even Colwyn Bay. An idyllic week in caravan, holiday camp or tent. Long carefree hours at the Sunset Valley camping site or the Golden Beach holiday village. Happy days at Happiland. And what delights we'd enjoy. But wait a minute — let Mary take up the story. She spent a week there with her fella and kept a diary. Not sure when — it could have been the late forties, the fifties, even the sixties or seventies. Over to you Mary.

Pictured outside their chalets, five Scouse lads having a great time at Butlin's in 1959. They just could be 'demob happy' though.

DIARY

Saturday
Got here about 4, Ronnie put the tent up and then we went into Rhyl for some milk and food (six tins of Newforge Irish stew). When we got back Ronnie put the tent up again.

Sunday
After Ronnie had strengthened the guide ropes (he'd tripped over them in the night looking for the toilet) we went to Talacre beach. It was great but Ronnie wouldn't eat the egg sarnies because of the wasps. He spent a bit of time on the guide ropes. Had some stew before we went for a few drinks in Prestatyn.

Monday
Met some people from Walton in the pub last night and had a real good bevvy. Stayed in bed late this morning as Ronnie fell over the guide ropes again and it was nearly 5 before he got the tent back up. The people in the next tent are dead snooty.

Tuesday
Rained all day but we went to a pub in Prestatyn in the evening. A different one from Sunday in case we bumped into those people from Walton again.

Wednesday
Ronnie suggested to the people in the next tent that we swapped a tin of Irish stew for something of theirs but they didn't want to know. They're from Birmingham, I think, and talk really funny. They gave Ronnie some extra tent pegs though.

Thursday

I won a Koala bear at Rhyl fair but Ronnie saw the same bear in a shop and worked it out that it had cost more to win mine. Ronnie sulked for a while but cheered up a bit when I went for some chips to go with the stew. Did a pub crawl in Rhyl and would you believe it, we met those people from Walton again.

Friday

Slept in late again and were woken up by the man in the next tent asking for his tent pegs back. We got back late last night and Ronnie got into the wrong tent and woke everybody up. We went for a drink at lunchtime. Ronnie put the tent back up in the afternoon.

Saturday

Going home today. Very windy this morning but I was impressed with Ronnie. He was dead quick getting the tent down and he gave the people in the next tent our last tin of stew. I thought it was dead nice of him, considering the way they've been all week. It's been a great week but won't be sorry to get home. Ronnie says never again . . . over and over.

Some of us even got to Butlin's, usually Pwllheli more exotically Skegness or Filey. Ringo made it for a season with Rory Storm and the Hurricanes. Some of us who got to Butlin's even made the escape committee but the combination of barbed wire, security guards, chalet patrols and redcoats usually ensured we stayed the week. Maplin's seems like a holiday camp compared to Butlin's in the 1950's. Still for about £12 you got accommodation, three meals a day and free entertainment. And women from Swadlincote or Newton-le-Willows. Or, for that matter, men too.

Table d'hôte, Butlins style. That chap with the googly eyes looks as though he could do damage with the sugar shaker. **Where** *are the women?*

BOTANICAL GARDENS

PAVILION & PROMENADE

MINIATURE RAILWAY
MARINE LAKE

EAST BEACH AND NEW PROMENADE

SWIMMING POOL

RHYL

ROCK GARDENS, EAST PROMENADE

CYCLING TRACK & PIER

BEACH &

POST CARD

Dear All,
   Having a great time, weather not too bad. Food excellent. We may climb the Great Orme tomorrow. We are both getting quite brown. Don't work too hard.
Ha, Ha.

     Mary and Ronnie
       xx

The Gang
Red Spot Distribution Section
'B' Shop Stores
English Electric Ltd.
Fusegear Division
East Lancs Road
Liverpool 10
England
(Ha)

A VIEW OF WALES

FANCY A DIP IN THE MURKY

To most Merseysiders, even though they may carry an abiding love for their eponymous river, the thought of swimming in it, *voluntarily*, would reduce them to tears of laughter. But through the years there have been many hardy souls who have done just that. Clubs such as the Mersey Open Water Swimming Club and the Seacombe Open Water Swimming Club have held regular races, and members of the Wirral Beach Patrol have been known to take the occasional dip. The youngest swimmer to conquer the Mersey was fourteen-year-old Adrian Simm from Prescot, who made the mile-and-a-quarter crossing from Langton Dock to New Brighton's Vale Park in just forty-five minutes.

The most regular swimming event on the river is the annual three mile police race which takes place between Seacombe and New Brighton. The only time the race has been cancelled was in 1981 when the demands of the Toxteth riots meant there was a shortage of competitors and officials. For many years the race was dominated by P.C. Williams, but in recent years P.C. Sean Kehoe has been unbeatable. The first lady to complete the swim was Policewoman Lesley Farlam who triumphed over the mighty Mersey in 1979 at the age of nineteen.

One of Merseyside's most remarkable contemporary swimmers is Mrs. R. M. Garzia of Liverpool 8. Mrs. Garzia only learned to swim when she was 51 years of age but less than two years later she decided to go for the Million Yards Swim as set out by the A.S.A. The regulations allow 5 years for the completion of this challenge but Mrs. Garzia needed only 15 months to complete it, mostly swam at the University pool and at Lodge Lane. She is now 60 but is still going strong, much of her swimming nowadays is for charity and she has added diving to her aqua repertoire.

YOU'RE NEVER TOO OLD

Competitive swimming is normally seen as the exclusive preserve of the very young, but Margaret Hohmann blew a hole in that theory when she celebrated her 32nd birthday, competing for Britain in the Seoul Olympics.

Better known as Margaret Kelly, this Bootle swimmer retired after a distinguished career, culminating in a relay silver medal in the Moscow Olympics. She returned to

Policewoman Lesley Farlam, from Moreton.

competitive swimming in 1986, following the birth of her first child, Robbie, and confounded those who suggested she would be unable to regain her former speed. Margaret admitted to such doubts herself.

"I didn't think about the Olympics because I didn't know if I really wanted to go. I was a bit half-hearted but my coach, Keith Bewley, kept me going."

The Wigan Wasps coach sent her training schedules through the post, so that she could train at the local pool in Nottingham, where she now lives. With her husband David and her neighbours taking it in turn to look after Robbie, she managed to find the time she needed to train.

After hearing of her selection for the British team she said:

"I'm delighted to have proved that it's not the end of the world when you have a baby, and pass the 30 mark."

The start of the 1961 Seacombe Swim.

WALK ON, WALK ON

Merseyside doesn't have the great tradition of Walking Days that can still be seen in many Lancashire towns. The nearest this particular tradition comes to Liverpool is down the road in Warrington, where the annual Walking Day has been celebrated for over 150 years. The Warrington Walks were started as a counter attraction to Haydock Races. It was, it is generally believed, the ideas of a devout pastor anxious to prevent his flock from having a flutter and becoming involved in the heavy drinking that invariably accompanied the races. There is a note in the parish church minutes of May 2, 1937 which states: "It was resolved that the anniversary usually held on Friday in Newton race week, should be celebrated in the same manner as last year."

There is also mention in the former National school records at Warrington dated June 3, 1934 that: "It was resolved that the children belonging to the National School should walk in procession on Friday next as is customary on the last day of the races.

The first Warrington Walking day tea took place on a mount behind the parish church, and during the procession the children's fathers jeered and booed — presumably because they resented any interference with the traditional family day's outing to the races, and their drinking.

Since then, Walking Day has become a time-honoured custom, the biggest day in Warrington's calendar.

Over the water in Neston a walk of a rather different nature takes place on the first Thursday in June, when members of the "Ladies' Club", as it is known locally, walk through the town.

The Neston Female Friendly Society was founded in 1814, to help poor and needy women at the end of the Napoleonic Wars. It was the first all-female welfare society in the country, and the first walk took place in 1815. For a small subscription, modest even then, the members were entitled to benefits for maternity, sickness and death.

All the women in the procession carry a white staff topped with sprays of flowers and ribbons. A special staff, called the Dispensation, is carried by the only man in the society, the secretary. The parade is headed by a banner carried by two men, with two boys to steady the ropes. The banner bears

Off for a day's walking in the Wirral at Whitsun 1955 are Joy Harding from Aigburth, Joyce Douglas from Speke. Margaret Watson from Childwall and Beryl Davies from Calderstones.

the society's motto; "Bear ye one another's burdens."

As well as the members, the parade includes members of the clergy, the mayor, other civic dignitaries, and a band.

The nearest Liverpool comes to an actual walking day is the "Glorious 12th", when 10,000 orangemen from Liverpool's 200 lodges march through the city en route for their annual trip to Southport. The annual outing celebrates King William's victory over James II, at the Battle of the Boyne, thus ending Stuart hopes of regaining the throne.

Neston Ladies walking in 1980.

The crowds gather in Moorfields to watch the 1952 Orange Lodge procession arriving at Exchange Station for the trip to Southport. In the picture can be seen Woodwards, the finest garden shop ever in the city, the aroma of flowers, fertiliser and potting compost, combined to produce a smell similar to the sweat-band of Walter Gabriel's hat. Further along from Woodwards is the 'Johnny Shop', more correctly known as Blakes Medical Supplies. Together with its companion shop in Cases Street, it was the scene of many a Scouse lad's first mumbled, blushing purchase of a 'packet of three'.

BARRY'S WALK ON THE WILD SIDE

In the shadow of Seaforth Container Base a young unemployed man sits munching his sandwiches, watching his fishing line snaking out across one of the lakes on the industrial wasteland caused by the construction of the huge dock. It is 1981 and the winds of recession on Merseyside are no less biting than the chill Irish Sea winds whipping across the North Mersey shore. But for Barry Jackson recession didn't mean depression. As he sat there fishing he looked around him and saw the building blocks of a nature reserve.

He armed himself with a notebook, pencil and plenty of patience. He noted plants, foxes, rats which nibbled at his sandwich box and bait tin. He recorded the birds — waders and ducks, the Canada geese, skylarks, kestrels, kittiwakes, and a large, black, scruffy cormorant feeding on the crabs and fish at high tide, such a regular to the dockers they nicknamed him Charlie.

After ten months' research he had compiled a dossier on the fauna and plants showing how the place could be developed as a reserve, tidied, trees planted, the two lakes cleaned, hides, pathways, and an information centre built. His plan was so detailed it even included the type and number of nails needed to build the observation hut.

It must have been a shock for the job centre staff when Barry marched in one day, clutching all his plans in a green folder asking for help. Eventually he arrived at the door of Merseyside Improvements Limited, a company set up by the Merseyside County Council to help the unemployed and regenerate the area, Barry was in business.

The Manpower Services Commission and the County Council backed Barry to the tune of £100,000, the dream became a reality. As work progressed the Seaforth Coastal

Nature Reserve, as it became known, picked up several major conservation awards, and botanist David Bellamy described the reserve as a site of potential international status. To the untrained eye the site may look little different than it did before but as Barry explains: "If you tidy the place too much you destroy the habitat of creatures like voles and mice which in turn provide the food for short-eared owls and kestrels.

"People get mixed up between a country park and a nature reserve. A park is for the public and the wildlife comes second. Here the wildlife comes first and the public come second.

"Some people think we have the birds in pens. We had a phone call from a woman in Crosby asking could we keep the geese quiet because they were waking the family early in the morning. Some people just don't understand the idea of a wild reserve."

By a monumental bureaucratic irony Barry was unable to become an employee of his own creation. The Lancashire Trust for Nature Conservation took over the running of the reserve, but were unable to afford any wages for employees. The MSC backed the scheme with enough cash for six full-time employees, but because Barry's time under the scheme had expired he could not be retained.

Barry Jackson moved on to pastures new, initially as a countryside ranger in Berkshire, and eventually as a countryside research officer with the Cheshire Landscape Trust. But Barry's legacy lies on the windswept stretch of the north Mersey coast at Seaforth, where one Merseysider's hobby became a dream, and then a reality, got give pleasure to thousands of nature lovers, and to secure one small segment of our environment for the future.

Barry Jackson (centre) with Ted Jackson of the Lancashire Trust for Nature Conservation and David Bellamy.

KISS ME GOODNIGHT SERGEANT MAJOR

The announcement from Liverpool F.C. was short and to the point. Liverpool F.C. have appointed their full back Ronnie Moran as captain for next season, 1959-1960. He succeeds John Wheeler, who has asked to be relieved of the captaincy.

'Bugsy' Moran was now part of the Anfield establishment.

Moran, an apprentice electrician with the Dock Board, made his first team debut in 1952 when he replaced Eddie Spicer at left back against Derby at the Baseball Ground. He had arrived at Anfield by a rather strange route. His potential had first been spotted by a postman who had the legendary T.V. Williams, then Anfield vice-chairman, later President, on his round. T.V., who always referred to Moran as "My Player," saw the potential in the Crosby schoolboy, and he pestered manager Don Welsh until Moran was at Anfield.

Like many young footballers of his day Ronnie Moran had his breakthrough into the big time delayed by National Service, initially he was stationed in Devon, which meant he saw little of Anfield until he was demobbed in July 1955.

Moran was always a competent player rather than a brilliant one although, as Bill Shankly did say, "I honestly believe that if I could have had Ronnie Moran under me at the same age I had Ray Wilson at Huddersfield, Ronnie would have played as often for England as Ray did."

His only representative honour came when he played for the English League against the Irish League in 1957.

His 339 appearances for Liverpool brought him only one Championship medal in 1964, his penultimate season. His last league game was at Molineux against Wolves in 1965, when he played in what was virtually a reserve side a few days before Liverpool beat Leeds in the Cup Final. This, however, was not his last game, Gerry Byrne was injured in the Final and Moran was drafted in to take his place in the ill-fated second leg in the European Cup Final against Inter Milan in the San Siro Stadium when Liverpool lost 3-0. Though his reaction to the Inter Milan programme line-up which had him down as May Moran, is unrecorded.

. . . .

Liverpool's right half, or right sided midfield player in the 1914 Cup Final was called — Tommy Fairfoul.

. . . .

After hanging his boots up Moran started his coaching career in charge of the A team, he became Central League trainer on the same day in 1971 that Bob Paisley became assistant manager and Joe Fagan took over as first team trainer. His ability and devotion to the Anfield cause saw him appointed chief coach in 1979. He became, and still is, the most successful coach of all time, having helped Liverpool to 21 major titles.

He's the man the players love to hate, the parade ground bully that brings out the best in his men with his aggressive approach. No fancy jargon, no complicated set plays, just hard work and concentrating on the basics, plus plenty of five-a-sides; the same training pattern that Shankly introduced.

Shanks once said of him: "If ever there was a one club man it was Moran. He was Liverpool through-and-through. He thought only in terms of Liverpool. I have heard it said he can only recognise one colour — red." As long as Ronnie Moran is at Anfield the Shankly spirit will never die. The sergeant major would simply not allow it.

Moran leads out the Reds in 1959.

No prizes for spotting the parrots in this pic, taken at the end of the 1983 Milk Cup Final.

Councillors McMillan and Kavanagh members of the Parks and Gardens Committee give an impromptu performance to test the acoustics at Calderstones Park's new open air theatre in 1947.

Prunella Stack demonstrating her keep fit methods at Anfield during a Health and Beauty pageant in 1938 in which 2,000 women took part.

Dancing the night away at St. John's Youth Club in 1958.

Liverpool and Birkenhead at Wembley. The Women's League of Health and Beauty Empire Pageant in 1939.

Calderstones theatre in 1950 and the revue "Flashes of 1950".

A summer morning in Sefton Park in 1961 and two youngsters visiting the Palm House.

"WARP FACTOR ONE, MR. CAMPBELL"

Kirkby's Carters' Arms pub on a wet November night in 1971 may not readily spring to mind as one of the region's artistic milestones but in its own way it was. It was the start of a week's engagements in Kirkby for the Ken Campbell Road Show, organised as the first venture of the Kirkby Arts Association. Billed as a "Wild Stunt Show", the evening quickly turned into a verbal battle between the actors and the more vociferous locals. This was Merseyside's introduction to the Campbell-style theatre of inspired lunacy.

Ken drifted in and out of the local theatrical scene, as his national and international commitments would permit. In 1976, miffed at the Everyman Theatre's Board for turning down his application for the post of artistic director, and at the same time excited by the city's capacity for nurturing eccentric sub-cultures, he formed the Science Fiction Theatre of Liverpool. Assisted by Chris Langham, Ken Campbell produced an epic cycle of plays called 'Illuminatus', at the Liverpool School of Language, Music, Dream and Pun in Mathew Street. The play with its bizarre mixture of fact and fantasy, had everything, the fall of Atlantis after being attacked by a yellow submarine, one of the main characters making love to a giant inflatable apple, and questioning why is there a Freemason's triangle on a dollar bill? It was seen by Peter Hall and transferred to the National Theatre in London, where it was cut down from its original 12 hours to something more manageable. Campbell's Association with the Liverpool School came to an end when he was putting

Prunella Gee (later Mrs. Ken Campbell) and Chris Langham, rehearsing 'illuminatus' at O'Halligans Parlour in Mathew Street, in 1976.

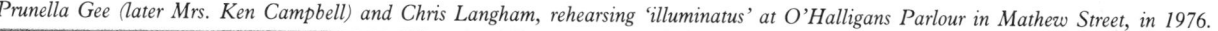

on an opera based on the H.P. Lovecraft horror classic, 'The Case of Charles Dexter Ward'.

Let Campbell take up the sad sequence of events: "There was an actor in the production, John Joyce, he spent all day in the toilet.

"In the end the toilet — the only one in the place — got blocked. We had a gay monk there who thought it had happened because my dog had dropped a bone down the pan. In the event the gay monk decided to unblock it. The resultant blockage travelled along the sewers to cause problems with the toilets in a nearby chain store.

"They discovered we were putting on an opera without a licence, as well as selling tea without a licecnce. So we are closed down."

In June 1980 he finally got the job he had coveted for so long, as artistic director of the Everyman Theatre. His first production was 'The Warp', which had originally been put on by the Science Fiction Theatre of Liverpool at the Edinburgh Festival, Campbell described it as: "A joyous mixture of music hall, science fiction, story-telling, sex and adventure."

Campbell is familiar to T.V. viewers as Alf Garnett's 'snotty' neighbour in 'In Sickness and in Health', and he made a big splash at Liverpool University's swimming pool, in 1986, when he organised Britain's first underwater rock show featuring local bands Lawnmower and the Bingo Brothers, as well as a scuba diving soprano, a snorkel string section, and a high diving trombone player.

CABBAGE HALL —WHAT'S IN A NAME

Cabbage Hall, now there's a funny name for a district, how did it come about. There are a number of theories.

1. In the 1870's there was an innkeeper called Jesse Turner who had a 7ft 9½in cabbage stalk hanging in the entrance hall of the inn. He had reputedly brought the stalk with him from Jersey.

2. The same innkeeper, Turner, grew huge cabbages in the adjoining field. The pub grub must have been really interesting, cabbage flavoured crisps, cabbage and onion sandwiches, cabbage and chips, cabbage pizzas, cabbage toasties . . .

3. A wealthy greengrocer in the area built a house which the locals found so pretentious they nicknamed it, Cabbage Hall.

4. A retired army colonel called Townsend lived in what is now known as Townsend Lane. The gateposts to his residence were adorned with stone pineapples. The local

children, never having seen pineapples, called them cabbages. Sounds reasonable to me.

5. Cabbaging was a term applied to the dubious tradesmen's practice of estimating in excess of the customers' material requirements, charging them accordingly, and pocketing the difference. This quaint local custom was raised to the level of an art form by a local tailor who habitually overcharged his clients for cloth and built a palatial home on the proceeds. Hence, Cabbage Hall; who knows in a different time the area might have been known as Burton's, Hepworth's or Weaver to Wearer.

The only corroboration to any of these theories came in 1967 when a retired civil servant living in Heswall wrote to the Liverpool Echo pointing out that he was Jesse Turner's grandson and he owned what was left of the monster cabbage stalk. He also produced the accompanying photograph which shows the famous cabbage on the inn sign.

"WON'T YOU LET ME TAKE YOU ON A SEA CRUISE . . ."

One of the Mersey's best-known visitors during the late sixties and early seventies was the cruise ship Uganda, but this was a cruise ship with a difference. The Uganda was a floating school, and school was never so much fun. The Uganda was built on the Clyde in 1950 for British India Steam Navigation (later merged with P&O) and was used on the run between Britain and East Africa. She was converted into a school ship in 1967.

The Uganda replaced the Dunera and the Devonia as floating classrooms, and although the introduction of these ships in 1961 was initially greeted with scepticism in many quarters, over the years their educational value was proved beyond dispute. Visits to Greece, Italy and the Middle East brought ancient history to life, and how better for children to learn the Christmas message than carol singing in the Holy Land? The summer trips into the Baltic with visits to Helsinki and Leningrad gave many youngsters a sociological insight into other cultures in a way that can never be bettered in the classroom. The kids certainly learned a lot, but they had a lot of fun too. The Uganda was the biggest mixed boarding school in the world, with bunks for 1,000 arranged in vast dormitories. 'Passion patrols' were laid on by the crew to curtail those whose youthful urges extended beyond the obligatory pillow fights. On one trip a wealthy Arab businessman tried to buy three attractive sixth form girls for his harem, and the Uganda once ran aground in Alexandria.

School cruising ended when the Uganda was requisitioned by the government to act as a hospital ship during the Falklands War in 1982, and a piece of icing on the educational cake disappeared from our children's lives forever.

THE MAGICAL MYSTERY STORE

In 1972, ten years after 'Love Me Do', and years before anyone else started to do anything about it, Jim and Liz Hughes began a small Beatles' museum. For years their Magical Mystery Store in Mathew Street was the only place in the city where visitors and local fans alike, could go for information about the Beatles, buy memorabilia, or just talk.

When Cavern Walks opened they moved into No. 9, the sign over the door read "Number 9 Dream". They organised a Beatles' convention in 1981, but as larger commercial interests saw the financial potential of the Beatles' linked tourism market, the competition became too fierce, and in 1984 they went out of business through a combination of cash shortages and health problems.

As a gesture of support Paul McCartney invited them down to London and presented them with an autographed scroll, in recognition of their 12 years' hard work.

Whatever benefits the city may gain in the future from the 'Beatle Business' it is hoped that Jim and Liz, the couple who kept the faith, will not be forgotten.

THE FUN NEVER SETS ON MERSEYSIDE

Frank was on his death bed and his wife asked him if he would like something special.

"I'd love a couple of salmon sarnies".

His wife came back and passed Frank his butties.

Frank finished them and then asked his wife why they weren't salmon?

"I couldn't open the salmon, love," she said, "I'll have to save that for the funeral".

And those famous Dockers . . .

Christian Barnard	"No overtime! Have a heart boss".
Dr. Jekyll	"I need a change".
The Martian	"What on earth's this about?"
The Storm Lamp	He never goes out.
The Weight Lifter	He waits while you lift.

1961 Cruise brochure.

B·I EDUCATIONAL AND HOLIDAY CRUISES

1961 CRUISING PROGRAMME

M.S. "DUNERA" 12,615 TONS
BRITISH INDIA STEAM NAVIGATION COMPANY LIMITED

FROM £28 INCLUSIVE

Excited youngsters leave on the 'Dunera' on August 4th, 1966.

ON YOUR BIKE

In about 1865 two Frenchmen walked into the Liverpool Gymnasium in Myrtle Street. They were wheeling an extraordinary looking machine which they called a velocipede. It was a mass of iron and wood, with iron tyres, it weighed some 80lbs. Among the people in the gymnasium that day was a small boy from Birkdale, called Alexander Alexander, he was so taken with these new machines that came to be known as bicycles, that at the first opportunity he purchased one and together with friends of a similar persuasion embarked on a series of adventures including, what must have been one of the first cycling tours of Ireland. Alexander was also the man who invented and patented curved handlebars for cycles.

In 1869 two members of the Liverpool Velocipede Club (an off-shoot of the Liverpool Gymnasium) made what must have been the first cycle ride from Liverpool to London, it took them three and a half days and they carried their luggage in carpet bags tied behind their saddles.

The bicycle put women on an equal footing with men, as long as they followed the social niceties of the age. In her handbook of bicycling for women published in 1890, the high priestess of cycling style, Miss L.C. Davidson stated: "A new world of enjoyment is unlocked to the woman who finds herself awheel."

She did, however, warn: "I must strongly caution every lady against taking a seat on a tandem, bicycle or tricycle in which there is a high connecting-rod between the handlebars and the frame; it is absolutely dangerous to do so, and a lady who is asked to share the danger of an imperfectly constructed machine of this nature, can form her own opinion of the gentleman(?) who would put her in such a position."

In warm weather Miss Davidson recommended "a little Fuller's earth dashed inside the stockings keeps the feet cool."

But Liverpool writer, Richard le Gallienne, summed it up for the ladies, when he said:

"When the day arrives on which woman shall call herself absolutely free, let the monument . . . take the form of an enthroned and laurelled bicycle."

Liverpool Velocipedes about to set off from Exchange Flags for North Wales, on June 1st, 1878.

Mr. and Mrs. Kenneth May and sons Paul and Timothy of Beechfield Road, Calderstones, about to board the ferry for a Whit weekend on wheels in 1961.

*Indoor cycling at the Liverpool
Eagle Road Cycling Club in 1958,
ladies champion
Joan Kershaw in the saddle.*

Causing a stir in Liverpool in 1936 on the new Triumph.

MEMORABLE MERSEYSIDE DAYS

In volume two we asked readers to write and tell us about their memorable Merseyside day. A lot of memorable days were recalled, here are just a few:

It is early in 1941, I am returning home after a day's work in The Temple in Dale Street. The air raid warning sirens have gone, it is dark. I turn off Garston Old Road into Duncomb Road. The sound of unsynchronised engines grows louder. Looking up I see a Heinkel III bomber at not much more than rooftop level appear, coming from the direction of the river. His bomb doors are open and incendiary bombs are cascading down. I dive over a low garden wall and hear the incendiaries bouncing around in Duncomb Road. One is burning on the other side of the low garden wall. I start scooping up soil from the garden border and throwing it onto the bomb. A lady comes out of the house and, bucket of water in hand, comes to help. A leaflet circulated only a couple of weeks previously warned that a new device had been fitted to incendiaries which caused them to blow up if touched by water. Just as the lady threw the bucket of water, I caught her arm and partially deflected it. Some of the water splashed on the bomb and it went up. My cherished office boy's suit caught most of it, fortunately none went onto my face.

I jumped around and beat out the places where my precious suit was falling apart, escorted the lady back into her house, and turned into Torrington Road for home. I was more scared of facing my mother with my ruined suit than of the bomb! Clothes were rationed by coupons and I had none left!

H.S. Leeming
Rhossdu
Wrexham

Regarding my most memorable Merseyside day, it was in 1949.

That was while courting my late husband Frank, we had arranged to meet at the Pierhead, as I lived in Walton and he was lodging in Wallasey.

After waiting hour an hour I thought I'd got it wrong and we must be meeting over the water, so I jumped on a ferry.

Halfway across the Mersey, another ferry passed us going to Liverpool and there was Frank on the deck. Arriving at Seacombe I thought what do I do now. We could end up doing this all night if he spotted me. But I didn't think he had, so I got the ferry back. You've guessed it, he did the same thing and we passed each other again in the middle of the Mersey. This time we waved and I stayed in Liverpool until he came back again.

What a way to spend an evening! Happy days.

Joan O'Rourke
Borehamwood
Herts

My most memorable day was in 1955 when the Reds were in the 2nd division (talk about the phoenix rising from the ashes). We beat Everton, a 1st division team, 4-0 at Goodison in the FA Cup. The day started in the Big Ben pub in Mount Vernon Street, (now part of the Royal Teaching Hospital car park). We then moved on to the Blue House by Goodison Park. I was with my mates, John Brereton, Jackie Harnwell, Kenny Eaton, Eddie Flynn, Joey Beadon and some other Reds fans from our area. In the "Blue House" we met up with a crowd of Irish Evertonians who had travelled from Dublin for the match. We had a few drinks with them, then about 2.40pm we strolled over to Goodison for the match. (It was an all ticket game, we had queued for 13 hours for our tickets at Goodison Park on a previous date from 11pm Saturday night until 12 noon the following day.) After the game and the fantastic win, we walked from Goodison to the "Big Ben" pub to celebrate, we took the Irish Evertonians with us. I had won £2-5 shillings (9 five bob bets). The Manager of the pub, Mick, an Irishman, had been holding the bets (all at even money, because they were made with mates or regulars in the pub). I went to the local chippy in Mount Vernon Street and bought 30 bobs worth of chips, fish, pies, pigs feet, etc. for our party including the Irish lads, to have a feed in the pub. (The Irish lads were made more than welcome because mine host, Mick and his wife Bridie were both from Southern Ireland). We had a great night, including a sing-song (weren't the pubs magic in those days), then a meal and sandwiches to eat on the boat. Later on, we walked the Dublin lads to the stop to get their transport to the Pierhead for their boat journey home. From the pub we got ale out, some of it in those giant brown stone jars and went to a do in the Gibney's house in Horsley Street. We celebrated far into the night. Our only worry was how to get a ticket for the next round of the cup.

Terry McEvoy
Chelwood Avenue
Liverpool 16

SAM CHEDGZOY

Sam Chedgzoy, one of Everton's finest ever wingers was responsible for a change in the laws of the game. In 1923 Sam took a corner, passed it to himself, dribbled along the goal line and scored. The following year the FA created a new rule whereby the taker of a corner kick may only play the ball once.

Sam, a speedy right winger, played for Burnell's Ironworks team, in Ellesmere Port, with Joe Mercer's dad before joining Everton in 1910. Sam's forte was being able to provide a good quality cross while running at full speed. His dynamic wing play earned him nine England caps, at a time when fewer internationals are played than nowadays.

He was a one-club man throughout his sixteen year career, his only break from Goodison came during the First World War, when he played for the Scots Guards against Germany.

In the summer of 1924 he went to Montreal for a summer coaching engagement. Sam was so taken with the Canadian way of life that when he finished with Everton in 1926 he emigrated to Canada, where he got a job with an insurance company. He continued playing soccer and turned out for a Montreal side against a Scottish touring team at the age of 50.

Sam, who died in Montreal in 1967 at the age of 78 was one of many fine footballers produced by Ellesmere Port, such as: Joe Mercer, Stan Cullis and Dave Hickson.

His son, Sydney, also a winger, was on Everton's books for a while, he also played for Tranmere Rovers, New Brighton, Halifax, Runcorn, Sheffield Wednesday and Swansea Town.

By a strange coincidence an Evertonian of the Chedgzoy era was responsible for another change in the FA's rulebook. Jack Kendall, an ex-Evertonian goalkeeper transferred to Lincoln City, was involved in a bizarre incident when he started throwing his cap at opposing forwards to put them off. Referees could find nothing to penalise him on, and as a result the rules were changed.

Sam Chedgzoy.

FORE

It was in 1937 that the late Frank T. Copnall, a portrait painter, trundled on to the links of the Royal Liverpool Golf Club with what is believed to be the first golf trolley.

Made locally to his own specifications, it ran on either pram or cycle wheels — nobody was quite sure which.

Initially it was a source of amusement for other golfers, it remained in service for many years, a lone forerunner of the mass-produced trollies of the post-war years.

As this 1949 picture taken at the Cheshire Ladies Tournament at Caldy Golf Club shows, the trolley is still enough of a novelty to be viewed with amusement. This particular golf cart was made for Mrs. Smith Barnes by her husband, to get round the shortage of caddies available for the event.

THE SCOUSEOLOGY PICTURE QUIZ

PQ1   What and where?

PQ2   Action at the Stadium in 1975 but who is 'on top'?

PQ3   An ordinary housewife doing her shopping in Liverpool in 1967? Or is it?

PQ5   That's Billy Wright on the right, but who is the Liverpool born footballer in the middle?

PQ4   Who are they and why are they so pleased with their plane tickets?

PQ6   Name the group.

PQ7 A limping Geoff Strong scores with a classic header against Celtic at Anfield in 1966 to put Liverpool into the European Cup Winners Cup Final. Billy McNeill's there, Murdoch No. 4, the Saint. But what was the score of the 1st Leg match?

PQ8 Mobbed in Liverpool, but who is it?

PQ9 Luton supporters? — the Lewis's hat department sales force? — Butchers going out on the town? No. — Who then?

PQ10 A delightful 1946 scene at a famous Liverpool landmark — Where?

PQ11 Who is the lady on the left? Scouseologists really should know by now!

PQ 13 The Tunnel entrance but what year?

PQ12 Any ideas at all?

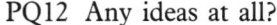

PQ 14   Where are they?

PQ 15   A Liverpool park aviary — what park?

PQ 16   Whitechapel in December, but what year?

PQ 17   It's 1944, Liverpool University, but what's going on?

PQ 18   England's narrowest house — where in Liverpool?

PQ 19 If you've seen the Scouseology calendar for 1989 you'll know who the young lad with the big smile in the middle is.

PQ 20 The bells of this church survived the blitz but were no longer rung from the tower but from the pavement. What church?

"Hey good lookin', what you got cookin'?"
I think this Scouse chef has ended up with a wet nellie if you ask me.

THE GOLBORNE BLACKSMITH

When Peter Kane went back to his corner, after being outpointed by Stan Rowan at Manchester in 1948, in a British title eliminator he said: "That's the end." It was his last bid to capture the only title he never won — a British Championship.

Born as Peter Cain in Heywood, his family moved to Golborne when he was three. He became a blacksmith, and always maintained that was what gave him his magnificent physique. Kane was world champion at flyweight and European champion at bantamweight, but that British title always eluded him.

He was a tremendous draw at the Stadium, where he did the bulk of his fighting. He was also very popular in France, particularly in Paris, where he was known as "le petit forgeron." Kane lost only a handful of decisions out of almost 100 contests spread over 14 years. He won his first 41 in a row, then came unstuck in his 42nd, when he was knocked out in the 13th round of his British and World title bout with Benny Lynch in one of the greatest fights in British boxing history. In a rematch with Lynch at Anfield he could only manage a draw. Lynch could not make the flyweight limit after that fight, and in September 1938 he fought Jackie Jurich for the vacant world title at Anfield. In a terrific finish Kane put Jurich on the canvas five times in the last six rounds, but had to be content with a points win. At 20 he was champion of the world. He lost his title to Jackie Peterson in 1943 and shortly afterwards left boxing for a couple of years.

He made a brave come-back in 1946 and was rewarded by winning the European bantamweight title in 1947.

But the British title remained just out of reach.

Cover Kane-Jurich programme.

Peter Kane with Sandy Powell, the entertainer, at the Hippodrome in Liverpool in 1937 studying news film of his successful fight with Jim Warnock.

THE FUN NEVER SETS ON MERSEYSIDE

Dad was in the pub on Christmas Day (when they opened) waiting for his two married sons. Ken and Ray arrived and Dad said to Ken.

"Pint of bitter, Son?".

"Just a half, Dad, I'm bloated with turkey. It was so big Cheryl and me had to force it into the oven".

Dad turned to Ray.

"Pint of bitter, lad?"

"Just a half, Dad, I'm bloated with goose. It was so big Carol had to cut it in half and cook it separately.

Dad ordered three halves of bitter and Ray turned to him and asked.

"By the way, Dad, what did you and Ma have for your Christmas dinner?"

Dad turned to him.

"Salt fish lad . . . Mind you it was so big we had to soak it overnight in Cornwallis Street baths".

SHOOTING STAR

For every amateur sportsman the Olympic Games must be the ultimate goal, with a gold medal as the impossible dream. But Garston G.P. Laslo Antal had no hesitation in turning down the chance of making it a reality in 1980, the year of the Moscow Olympics. Dr. Antal had three opportunities to go. As a competitor, as a coach, and as a medical officer.

Not only did he not take part, he also played a significant role in persuading the British shooting team to withdraw. As one who had escaped to the West, when the Russians invaded Hungary, the moral issues involved, including the occupation of Afghanistan, made his decision an easy one.

Not only did he miss out on taking part, but he also missed the very real chance of a medal, since the powerful American and West German teams had already withdrawn.

Laslo Antal, a British Champion in the Free pistol shooting event, had come a creditable 12th in the Montreal Olympics, only 8 points behind the winner who set a new world record. Free pistol shooting is a lot harder than it sounds, and we'd back Dr. Antal against Clint Eastwood any day.

Here's how to practice the physical side of an Olympic shoot without a pistol. Take your ordinary household iron, weight about three pounds. Go outside and raise it at arm's length. Hold it, and your whole body, absolutely rock steady for 30 seconds, focusing on a small object about 50 metres away. Repeat 75 times over a period of two and a half hours.

That's the easy part. If you were doing it for real you would be aiming at a bull's-eye 5 centimetres in diameter (that's one quarter the width of this page), 50 metres away, or about half the length of a football field.

Each competitor is allowed 15 'sighting' shots and 60 which count. On form Dr. Antal would hit the bull with nearly every other shot, the remainder would land in the next ring.

He can give us our 'shots' any day.

NEVER ON A SUNDAY

On May 20th 1947 the citizens of Liverpool went to the polls, not for the normal May local government elections, but for something far more important. Should you be able to go to the pictures on a Sunday?

The question of Sunday opening for cinemas in the city was not new, as long ago as 1930 Sidney Silverman had applied to the justices on behalf of the Merseyside Film Society, for permission to exhibit "Shanghai" and "The Girl with the Hatbox" at the Hope street cinema. In nearby Southport six cinemas were already opening on the Sabbath, but Liverpool still had another seventeen years to go.

In the Thirties cinemas were allowed to open on two Sundays a year if part of their proceeds went to charity. The first to take advantage of this was the Burlington Cinema in Vauxhall Road in 1932, which showed "Song of My Heart", with all the takings going to Our Lady's Church, Eldon Street. At that time 20 per cent of takings, at least, had to go to charity and that was enough to deter most cinema operators, later the charity cut was dropped to 10 per cent and as a result most picture houses opened for the permitted two Sundays each year.

Regular Sunday opening began in June 1941 under the auspices of Defence Regulation 42B for the benefit of the Armed Forces, and remained in operation until the 1947 poll, when the wartime ruling expired. A high turnout, with 23 per cent of the eligible electorate voting produced a majority in favour of Sunday cinema by 73,000 to 47,000.

Laslo Antal.

CHINATOWN — NORTH WALES

We all know the old joke; a Chinaman flags a taxi down on Berry Street and asks the driver to take him home, the driver replies: "Sorry pal, I haven't got enough petrol to go all the way to China." In the summer of 1958 it actually happeneed. A fleet of taxis and coaches were used to transport hundreds of local Chinese, including 120 children to North Wales, to work as extras on the film 'The Inn of the Sixth Happiness'.

In the hills above Beddgelert, close to the village of Nantmor, the Chinese walled city of Wang Chang was re-created.

For the children it was more like a holiday than work, they were well fed and four teachers from Caernarvonshire Education Authority looked after their schooling. One day the star of the film, Ingrid Bergman, who played the missionary Gladys Aylward, bought up an ice-cream seller's whole stock for the children.

The children had been 'found' by Chris Davis from Greasby, who went from house to house in 'Chinatown' photographing all the children. Chris, who had considerable experience of working in the Chinese community, then submitted the photographs to the film's director, Mark Robson, who then selected the types he wanted.

The climax of the filming was the bombing of the city of Wang Chang. This was accomplished without accident or injury to any of the children, as was the rest of the filming. The only casualties were a party of rubber-necking sightseers whose car overturned into a ditch.

RUNNING AND WALKING FOR PARLIAMENT

As our M.P.s become ever more faceless, it is the individualists we remember. More and more our representatives face each other from behind the sandbags of prejudice, only popping up to throw the occasional handful of wet dogma in the general direction of the opposition.

Ernest Marples, M.P. for Wallasey for 29 years, was one of the most colourful characters ever to grace the House. He is well remembered as the man who earned the wrath of the nation's motorists by introducing yellow lines and parking meters, among other things, during his six years as Minister of Transport. Remember the "Marples Must Go" stickers?

A man of legendary energy, at his constituency surgeries he would write letters by hand as constituents were outlining their problems and give them the letters to post, to the appropriate Minister or department, on the way out.

He was a keep fit enthusiast, and one of the first public figures to take up jogging, his morning route in London used to take him around the Royal Parks, following a route marked by the Royal trees — 55 yards at a trot, 55 at a brisk walk. He was an enthusiastic cyclist, and often arrived at the House of Commons on his bike.

Another local M.P. who gave us a smile over the years was Toxteth's Dick Crawshaw who represented the area from 1969 until 1981, when he left Labour and joined the SDP, ultimately becoming the SDP's first life peer, with the title of Baron Crawshaw of Aintree.

When not serving his constituents, Dick Crawshaw, always an individualist, was busy with his hobbies of long-distance walking and free-fall parachuting. As well as raising thousands of pounds for charity, particularly the NSPCC, with his walks, he also set a world record of 255 miles non-stop walking, at Aintree racecourse in 1972.

Typical of Crawshaw's life, he died just before he was due to take part in a fund raising regatta on the Thames in 1986.

A happy group of Chinese children on a take-away in North Wales.

BIG JOHN

Marples must go — to the Commons in 1952.

Scousers are notoriously cynical and don't always take everything at face value. John L. Sullivan's appearance in an exhibition match at Hengler's Circus, in March 1888, nearly ended in a riot since the crowd didn't believe that Sullivan was the genuine article.

A contemporary account continues the tale . . .

"Amidst a scene of great uproar, Jem Mace, who was acting as referee, assured the assembled company that the man before them was John L. Sullivan. Mr. Phillips, Sullivan's manager, confirmed this assurance, and said there were a number of people present who could substantiate his statement. Notwithstanding this, a number of the audience still persisted in saying it was not the right man, and on this Sullivan himself attempted to speak, but for a few moments was unable to obtain a hearing.

When he succeeded in making his voice heard, however, the suspicions of the unbelievers appeared to be at once dispelled. He explained that he had shaved off his moustache, which had made a change in his physiognomy. He referred at some length, to his match with Mitchell, which he designated as a foot race, and his inability to arrange a match with Jem Smith. He also alluded somewhat bitterly to some remarks in a sporting paper relative to his private affairs, upon which he refrained from expressing an opinion.

After some further remarks he thanked his hearers for their kind attention and the hearty applause with which they had greeted him in the course of his speech, and having completely satisfied them that he was the genuine man he went on with the sparring exhibition."

The first German tourists arrive on Merseyside. These days their kit bags would probably be sponsored by Adidas.

Bellew   Hey Youngie, that guy with the glasses looks remarkably like . . .

Young   It is him, Alderman Graham Reece, he was in Scouseology Two meeting Joe Louis.

Bellew   Proper little poser wasn't he. Did he meet everyone famous who came to Liverpool in those days?

Young   Either that or he was well in with the Echo's photographers.

Bellew   What's he up to this time?

Young   He's meeting Afrique, who was appearing at the Pavilion Theatre.

Bellew   Afrique eh. What was he? A hypnotist or a strong man act knowing the Pivvy.

Young   No idea, Bellew, but he's congratulating our friend Graham Reece on Liverpool's first luxicabs in 1938.

Bellew   He must have been a good act anyway. That's the Adelphi he's staying at and that number plate it's almost the same as the one you've got now Youngie.

Young   By the way Bellew its poseur from the French . . .

N.B.   *Afrique was in fact Southport born Alec Whitkin who was a leading opera singer at Covent Garden (he would sing in five languages). He then turned to the variety stage and was billed as the 'World's Greatest Impressionist' and included impressions of Stalin, Montgomery and Eisenhower in his act. Afrique's impersonation of Churchill at a London theatre was in the presence of the Wartime leader and the impersonation had Churchill on his feet giving the familiar two-fingered gesture. Perhaps he didn't like impressionists.*

Two of Liverpool's unsung sporting heroes. Liverpool University shot putt champion D. J. Byrne doing his famed 'how to clear a crowded bowling green in seconds' act. Leading amateur goalie of the thirties, H. J. Drury of Marine A.F.C., who used to crease opposing forwards with his shorts.

Competitors in an early Liverpool Marathon in 1929 receive a briefing at the Stadium before the event.

And afterwards, on your marks, set . . .

GO.

92

The start of the 1982 marathon.

THE THIRD MAN

October 1st, 1958, backstage at the Essoldo, Birkenhead, two British rock legends, Marty Wilde and Billy Fury together with . . . with who? — you may well ask.

It was an historic night, Marty Wilde, Kim's Dad, was appearing in the "Oh Boy" show and it was the night of Billy's first big chance.

Within a few months Fury was to have his first hit record, "Maybe Tomorrow", before "Colette" became his first top tenner in March 1960. At the time of that chart success Billy was touring Britain with the ill-fated Gene Vincent-Eddie Cochran tour which tragically ended with Cochran's death on April 17th. That famous rock tour has been brilliantly dramatised by Bill Morrison and researched by Spencer Leigh whose "Be Bop A Lula" was the highlight of the 1988 Liverpool Playhouse season, helped by the superb playing of the principal characters Andrew Schofield, Tim Whitnall and Gary Mavers.

But back to the picture. Who is the young aspiring rock star on the right? We're afraid we're going to keep you in suspense a little longer. He didn't make it as a rock star but if you still want to know who he is, check on page 122.

MERSEY POP TEASERS

1. Which group first top tenner was Enola Grey and on what label was it recorded?

2. Who recorded the album 'What Price Paradise?'

3. What artiste had a double hit with Hot Diggity/Gal with the Yaller Shoes?

4. Cryin Shames had a hit with "Please Stay" a highlight of the Mersey beat era. But who wrote the song?

5. What group were Billy Kinsley and Tony Crane the two lead singers?

6. Who was the first American singer to record a Lennon/McCartney song?

7. Who was Peter Flannery better known as?

8. What was the title of Ken Dodd's first top ten hit?

9. Who recorded 'The Story of the Blues' in 1982?

10. Who is the Liverpool born singer who appears on Rick Wakeman's suite 'The Gospels'?

Answers on page 122

Liverpool cult rocker, Albie Donnelly at Maxim's in Paris. Albie and his group Supercharge played at the world famous restaurant especially for Tina Onassis at her wedding reception.

Meccano's robot salesman travelled as far as Japan to sell the Company's products.

FOR LITTLE HANDS
PLASTIC MECCANO
BIG PIECES WITH BRIGHT
COLOURS MAKE MODELES
EASY TO BUILD EXCITING
TO LOOK AT
LTD LIVERPOOL 13
ENGLAND

The home of Newfooty, Hornby trains and of course Meccano as this card from Poland confirms.

THE FUN NEVER SETS ON MERSEYSIDE

Mrs. Wilson was talking to her neighbour about her son's early days at the 'Inny' after passing the scholarship "He's doing very well," she said proudly, "doing all sorts of foreign languages, he speaks Latin like a native".

Harry and Richard had been on holiday together to Butlin's and had met a couple of girls from Liverpool.

"Mind you," said Richard, "you can tell a girl from Liverpool".

"Yes" replied Harry, a little wistfully.

"But you can't tell her much".

The two Evertonians were looking a little despondent as they looked at Liverpool's lead in the race for the 1988 championship. Just then, a Liverpudlian pal came up waving an Echo.

"I see you're lot have bought Steve Davis".

The two Evertonians looked at him increduously (or at least a little surprised).

"What for," one asked.

"Well, you'll need snookers if you're gonna win the League now!"

Members of the Liverpool women's band Gillian Kidger of Fairfield, Linda Dron of Dovecot, Jean Hay of Edge Hill, Kathleen Daley of Old Swan, Sylvia Hurley of West Derby and Marilyn Aspinall of Roby pictured in 1959.

BLOWING OUR TRUMPETS — AS USUAL

Sometimes Merseysider's crossed the water to play as this queue for the Isle of Man boat during T.T. week in 1947 suggests.

12-year-old Lawrence Nicolson the youngest member of the 7F Squadron Band and a pupil at Dingle Vale School, chosen to play at the Farnborough Air Display in 1950.

THE DOOG

If you were one of the 52,293 packed into Goodison Park on August 19th, 1961, you may remember the match for something other than the result. As Everton's opponents, Aston Villa, took the field, the crowd were initially silent, then broke into gales of laughter. Derek Dougan, Villa's new centre forward signed from Blackburn Rovers for £15,000 to replace Inter Milan-bound Gerry Hitchens was sporting a rather strange haircut, in fact it wasn't really a haircut at all, because he had no hair, his head had been shaved.

The 'Doog' responded to the hoots of the crowd by going down to the goalmouth and doing an Indian war dance around the goal. His team-mates promptly nicknamed him Cheyenne.

After the match, Joe Mercer, asked him why he had done it. He told him that he had asked the barber how much it was for a haircut. The barber said it was four and nine pence, and a shave would be one shilling and nine pence. So Derek said; "I'll have a shave, then" — and had all his hair shaved off.

The 'Doog' was a natural rebel. In his first match for Villa, a friendly, he played with his socks turned down and no shinpads, it was big Derek's gimmick. His angry manager Joe Mercer told him: "If you want to do something unusual, score goals!"

SUNDAY BEST

When Steve Taylor (2) and Alex Bakeman popped in the goals for Liverpool Sunday league club, Lobster, at Haig Avenue, Southport on May 6, 1979, they were starting a tremendous run of success for Merseyside clubs in the F.A. Sunday Cup competition. On that day Lobster ran out 3-2 winners over Carlton from London, to capture the Shah of Persia trophy.

Merseyside clubs dominated the tournament during the eighties, with clubs like Fantail, who won the competition in 1980 and 1981, Dingle Rail who won in 1982, and Eagle in 1983 (Eagle lost in the final the following year) carrying all before them.

But there is a price to be paid for success. In 1986 when Birkenhead's Avenue carried off the trophy in front of a 2,552 crowd at Prenton Park, their earnings, once the F.A. had taken out all the match expenses amounted to the princely sum of . . . £1.13. Probably less than Ian Rush tips his hairdresser.

The 'Doog' at Goodison — 1961.

PUTTING ON THE RITZ

It wasn't quite the Odeon Leicester Square, but in November 1949 the Ritz cinema in Birkenhead staged a passable imitation of the Royal Command film performance, except for the fact that there was no royalty present. The special performance of that year's royal film, "The Forsythe Saga," starring Greer Garson, Walter Pidgeon and Errol Flynn, was put on in aid of the Cinematograph Trade Benevolent Fund. The pouring rain did little to dampen the enthusiasm of the crowds in the street outside, who came to see movie favourites such as, Gregory Peck, John McCallum, Bebe Daniels, Ben Lyon, Margaret Lockwood and Valerie Robson.

Inside, after watching a film of scenes at the real royal film show, the stars gave an impromptu concert on the cinema's stage.

THE FUN NEVER SETS ON MERSEYSIDE

Mary and Pat were in the Majestic watching the Pathe News about Cowes regatta.

"A yacht," said Mary to her friend.

"Yes," said Pat, "why don't we get a couple of lolly ices to cool us down".

Derek was describing the size of the guy who had picked on him.

"He was huge," said Derek, "he had a head like a lodging house cat".

COME IN NUMBER SEVEN

"What happened Col?"
Well it was a wet night, really wet, the buses had stopped running and I couldn't get a cab. Anyway, this fella at the Albert Dock said I could borrow his boat so I thought "Great". The route was a bit tricky though. I had to go up Great Mersey Street, past Atlantic House, across Seel Street, down Water Street . . . You've got the drift by now . . .
Car Salesman, Colin Brown, in June 1966 with the 30 foot ships' lifeboat he converted into a luxurious 6 berth cabin cruiser in six months. The cruiser was taken by lorry from Anfield to its mooring in Rhyl.

NEW TREASURER TO EM-BARK ON REFORMS

Mutley the Alsatian was voted by Liverpool University Students their Union's Treasurer in February 1987. What's more, he was only just pipped at the post by Jill Harris to the position of President. Pictured here with his owner, John Woodward, he was quoted, through an interpreter of course, as saying that despite his election the University was not going to the dogs but that certain reforms would be implemented. Maybe some extra lamp posts on Campus.

THE FUN NEVER SETS ON MERSEYSIDE

The bus inspector on the 17D was looking closely at Tommy's ticket.
"Where did you get on?" he asked.
Tommy turned and pointed to the conductor.
"Just by where he's standin'," he said.

MORE FAMOUS DOCKERS
The Bird Doctor   "This Lark's no good".
Maid Marian   "Two nights will save me".
Dope Peddler   He's got a car, but cycles to work.
Broken Boomerang He never comes back.
Cinderella   Always leaves at 5 to twelve.

WHALE OF A TIME

The footballing Students of Liverpool College are framed within these old whale jawbones in the sylvan setting of their final resting place. The bones once belonged to an ex-whaling skipper who had a cottage in Ibbotsons Lane, Sefton Park, and the jaws formed an arch in his garden. He swore it was the last Greenland whale in the world.

Liverpool's thriving whaling trade existed from about 1745 to 1820 and in 1775 Richard Kent launched Liverpool's first whaler, The William, built of English oak which ploughed the Arctic seas for over 50 years.

Liverpool had close links with Captain Scott's ill-fated Antarctic expedition. The whaler Terra Nova used by Scott in 1911 was lent to him by the Bowrings — the well-known Liverpool shipping family.

EN GARDE

In the fifties and sixties before Liverpool Eight was re-named Toxteth, people walking along Catherine Street were often surprised to hear the clash of steel rising up from one of the basements. The sounds of the foil, epée and sabre were coming from Professor Vladimir Zaaloff's fencing academy.

Liverpool's immigrants have come from far and wide, but the Russian-born fencing instructor's route to his adopted home was one of the strangest of all.

Zaaloff was born into a wealthy Georgian land-owning family, and like his father who was a general in the Russian Imperial Army he decided upon a military career. While he was at military school he won a number of fencing championships, and on receiving his commission he was commanded to become fencing instructor to Prince Alexis, son of the last Czar. The First World War intervened, and the young Zaaloff was sent off to the front. He was wounded and captured. After being unconscious in a German prison hospital for nine months, he managed to escape and made his way to neutral Denmark and eventually home to Russia.

The severity of his injuries meant he could not return to active service, he was transferred to the Diplomatic Corps, and was sent first to Copenhagen and then to the Russian Embassy in London. While he was there the Revolution took place, and his father was murdered by the Bolsheviks. After the Revolution Zaalof couldn't go back to Russia, and when Britain finally recognised the new Soviet government he had to leave the embassy.

Alone, in a foreign land, Zaaloff decided to make his way in the world by setting up a fencing academy. In order to finance his enterprise he turned of his second love, the stage, he produced a number of shows with Russian Ballet and Cossack dancing. A skilled balalaika player he once formed a quartet which appeared at Buckingham Palace and at Windsor for the benefit of the Royal Family. Eventually he was able to open his academy near Piccadilly Circus, and everything went well for him until he was bombed out during the Blitz. After the War he had difficulty in finding premises and the Amateur Fencing Association approached him to come to Liverpool, to give sport in the area a shot in the arm.

In 1947 he opened his fencing academy in Catherine Street and was part of the cosmopolitan Liverpool Eight scene for many years. As well as the private lessons he gave there he was also fencing instructor to Liverpool and Manchester Universities. In January 1968 he was elected life member of the British Fencing Academy in recognition to his service to the sport. Sadly a month later Zaaloff died, robbing the city of an urbane educated man whose wide-ranging interests included angling, bridge, music and dancing, particularly ballet.

In fact he acted as interpreter for the Bolshoi Ballet on one of their trips to Britain.

In spite of living most of his life in this country he never lost his strong Russian accent, and his wife used to regularly tell him: "Zaaloff, you've been here for over forty years but your English is still bloody awful!"

The Zaaloff thrust.

ALBERT'S TURKISH DELIGHT

Playing the piano is a pleasant and relaxing pastime but for one nineteenth century scouser it was his passport out of a Turkish jail. Albert Quilliam trained as a railway engineer, and when Turkey was building railways, Albert was one of many British engineers working on them.

The Turko-Armenian war flared up and unfortunately for Albert and the rest of the Brits, we sided with Armenia. As a result all the British workers were imprisoned.

Around that time the Sultan of Turkey had a pipe organ installed in his palace but it wouldn't work. The call went out to the jail to get one of the imprisoned engineers to have a look at it, and Albert was taken from the prison to the palace. Not only could Albert repair the organ but he could also play if after a fashion.

The Sultan was so pleased he asked what Albert would like as a reward. Not unnaturally he asked for his freedom, but this was refused, instead he was offered all sorts of favours including the delights of the harem. *He refused.* (Obviously more willpower than your average Scouseologist, either that or he was working for a Sunday newspaper at the time).

Eventually he was given his freedom on condition that he became a Moslem and build a mosque on his return home. This he did, with the aid of a few bob from the Sultan, and he became a well-known figure in the city. He rode a white horse and habitually dressed in robes and quickly earned the nickname 'Sheik'. There was great consternation at his funeral when three women turned up claiming to be his wives.

EXCUSE ME, HAS ANYONE HANDED IN A RUBBER SKELETON?

Auctions are many people's favourite way of passing time, and the real value-for-money auctions are those lost property sales where you can pick up an umbrella for a few pence, or even a pair of football boots or s spare set of false teeth.

The number and range of items handed in to British Rail, the police, MPTE and other bodies, on Merseyside over the years, is quite amazing.

The umbrella comes top of the list, naturally, but what about a rubber skeleton, a bag of turnips, or an artificial leg. If none of those are to your liking you could always put a bid in for a tent, a wheelbarrow, or a baby kangaroo skin. HONEST WE'RE NOT MAKING THESE UP. Still nothing to suit you, how about six dozen miniature Christmas trees, a copy of the Koran, or a trombone. No? Some people are never satisfied, there's still the World War I gas mask, the Merchant Navy officer's uniform, the three foot high statue of Christ, the blood pressure gauge, the 30 piece dinner set, not forgetting the voodoo doll, or the very well worn copy of Spencer Davis: 'Keep On Running'. How do people lose all these things? The list is endless. There's the . . . . Now where DID I put that list?

Aladdin's Cave, sorting out lost property at Hatton Garden for the half yearly sale of items left on Corpy buses in 1958.

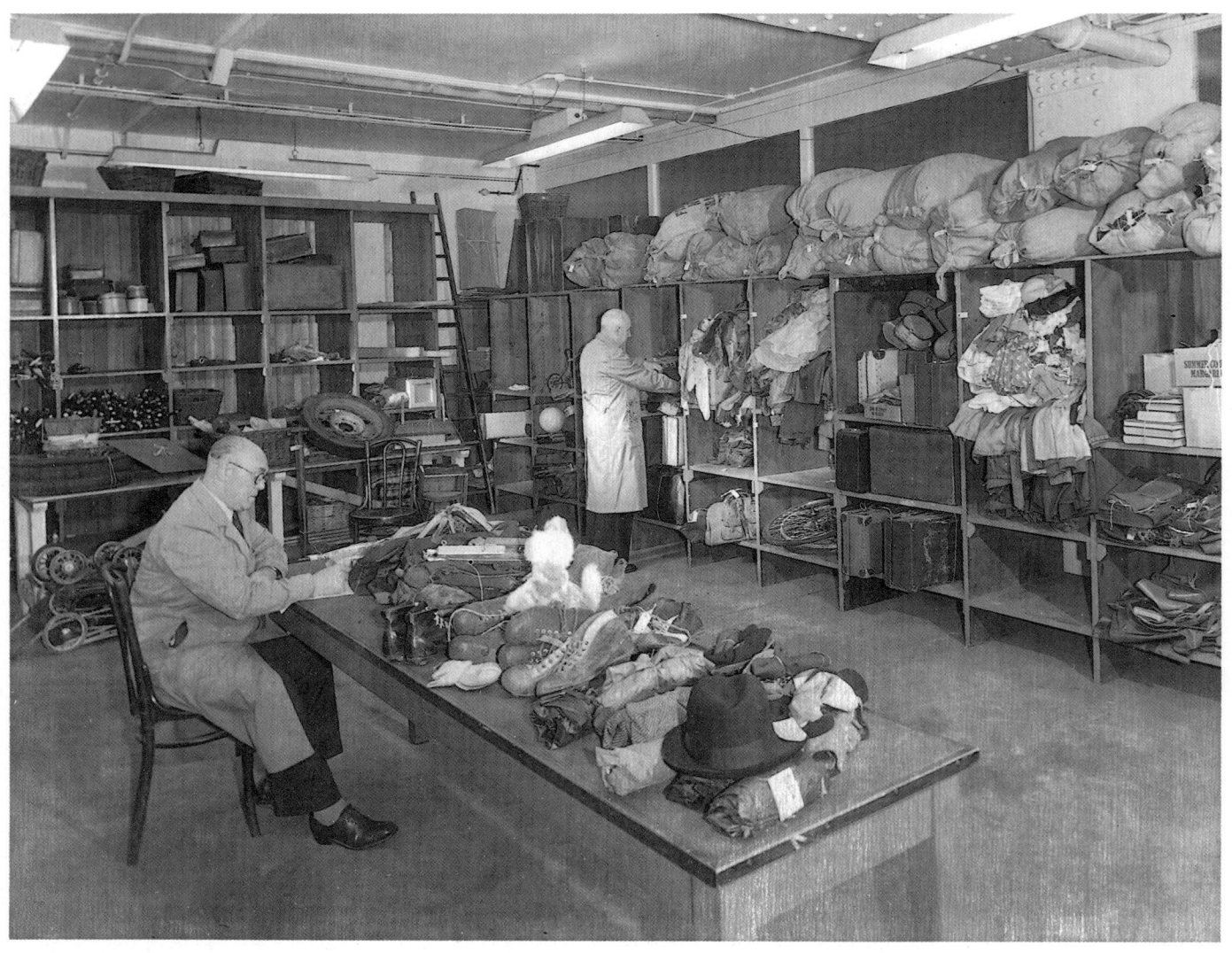

THE LAST DAYS OF THE SHAKESPEARE

The second weekend in March 1956 saw plenty of activity on the news pages of the daily press; Archbishop Makarios was being deported from Cyprus, the famous goalkeeper Sam Bartram (whose face seemed to figure on the cover of every other issue of Charles Buchan's Football Monthly), was making his last appearance at the Valley for Charlton, and Britain ruled the skies with the Fairy Delta II regaining the world airspeed record for Britain with a speed of 1,132 mph.

On that Saturday the great Len Shackleton was destroying Everton single-handed, leading Sunderland to a 2-1 win at Goodison, while Liverpool were cruising to a comfortable 5-0 victory away at Barnsley. Lost on the inside pages of the local papers was the story of the last night of music hall at the Shakespeare. The bill was headed by Rob Wilton, who had made his stage debut at the Shakey in 1900, when he was paid the princely sum of £2.00 for a week's run, in W. W. Kelly's "Royal Divorce".

The Shakespeare opened in August 1888, and after many successful years as a straight theatre it eventually became one of Liverpool's best known music halls. It was the city's premier pantomime theatre, and was the first to bring a Drury Lane panto to the area. The great George Robey was one of the most popular panto performers and Liverpool's Maggie Duggan was a regular principal boy. The Shakey has an obscure claim to fame in panto lore, being the first theatre to put on a production of Cinderella with the role of Dandini being taken by a man, John A. Warden.

More noteworthy was the fact that the Shakespeare was the first theatre in Britain to convert from gas lighting to electricity. The twice nightly variety shows started in 1932, and only the blitz had managed to bring down the curtain, until that March night in 1956.

The Shakey then became the Pigalle Theatre Club, but this lasted less than a year. Following the failure of the Pigalle the Shakey enjoyed two years of theatrical glory (and financial disaster) as the New Shakespeare Theatre, it was started in 1957 by the American actor/producer, Sam Wanamaker. Backed by the inherited wealth of his partner, Anna Deere Winman, another American, Wanamaker quickly set about establishing a reputation for excellence, and initially success seemed assured.

One of Wanamaker's most notable productions was Tennessee Williams' controversial play "The Rose Tattoo". Williams' steamy saga of love and lust, set in a village of Sicilians along the Gulf Coast between New Orleans and Mobile, had been banned by the Lord Chamberlain (remember him?), but protracted negotiations between Wanamaker and the authorities saw the play eventually put on, in November 1958, at first only for club members, but later for the general public.

The great Rob Wilton, centre stage next to Dave Morris wearing the boater (and Joe Gladwin next to him), leads the singing of 'Auld Lang Syne' before the final curtain when the Shakespeare closed on March 10th, 1956.

Rob, Dave and manager Peter Jackson see the irony of the poster on the Shakespeare's last night.

It's 1958 and it's ballroom dancing at the 'Shakey'.

Wanamaker and Anna Deere Winman celebrate the opening.

Sam Wanamaker and Lea Padovani in rehearsal for 'The Rose Tattoo'.

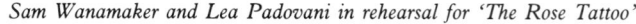

Early the following year the production, headed by Wanamaker himself and Italian movie star, Lea Padovani, made a triumphant transition to the West End. The only member of the cast not to travel to London was Blackie the goat, who had been enjoying his nights treading the boards, while on leave of absence from Southport Zoo. Doubtless he was replaced by some inferior southern goat.

Unfortunately for Wanamaker the financial winds began to blow chill. Anna Deere Winman withdrew her support, and returned to America, she died in March 1963 following a fall at her Bermuda home, and in February 1959 the theatre closed.

After four years of argument and discussion the Shakey re-opened as a luxurious night spot, with cabaret, dancing and a casino, but in November 1963, only two weeks after the opening, the place was wrecked by fire. Closed for nearly three years it was re-opened, yet again, in September 1966, following a £175,000 face-lift.

The interior had retained many of the original features but now the swinging sixties' patrons could take their pick of three restaurants, three bars and a lounge, as well as watch the cabaret. In the basement was the Mexican bar, in the auditorium the 60-foot long Promenade Bar — probably the longest in Liverpool at the time — and the 'gods' was Kanaka Jim's, a south sea island-inspired bar, of wicker chairs, plastic palms and witch doctor masks. Meals ranged from 12s 6d in the cheapest restaurant to 32s 6d, (37s 6d on Saturdays) in the more expensive French restaurant. The opening night's bill featured Edmundo Ros and his band, Libby Morris and Roy Castle.

For the next ten years the Shakey provided us with lavish entertainment, and behind the scenes drama, which saw ownership and finances juggled with all the aplomb of a one-armed blind man with Parkinson's Disease.

In 1971 boxing returned to the theatre for the first time since December 1931, and two of the fighters who appeared on the card that night, Ernie Roderick and Tom Bailey were in the audience to see Harry Scott fight the Frenchman, William Poitrimol. The cabaret between bouts was provided by Dave Allen, W. Barrington Daulby being unavailable.

The last act of the Shakey was played on March 21, 1976, when the building was completely gutted by fire, but the last ten years of the theatre's life had been as eventful as any that had passed before.

The Shakey, with the ever-present and always outrageous Pete Price as front-man, brought a string of top names to the city; Frankie Vaughan, Freddie Starr, Georgie Fame, Olivia Newton John, Sacha Distel, Johnny Ray, Dorothy Squires and hundreds more, from the ridiculous, Millican and Nesbit, to the sublime, Tommy Cooper, who on one appearance had trouble with the hydraulic stage when it failed to rise to its full level, and stuck halfway, leaving only Tommy's head and fez visible, he went right through his act, just like that.

Eleven days after the rain soaked Sunday morning which saw the final blaze, the Liverpool City Council Building Surveyor donned his black cap, and pronounced the Shakey officially dead. The building was damaged beyond repair.

The date? April 1st.

It's 1963 and the Shakey is now a plush cabaret club. Jimmy Edwards and Tina Scott join the joint managing director of the Robley Group, Ted Roberts, in a toast.

The great Paul Robeson in Liverpool at the New Shakespeare in 1958.

The finale. Liverpool entertainer, former Shakespeare compére and afficianado Peter Price hopes that the famous Shakespeare bust will be saved.

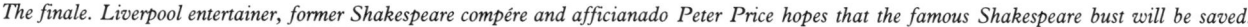

SEE YOU, JIMMY

One of the highlights of the Liverpool social calendar in the fifties and early sixties, was the annual Highland Ball, at St. George's Hall. The photograph shows the Grand March at the 1954 ball, the Lord Mayor, Alderman W. John Tristram is in the front rank, but most of the noise must have come from what a contemporary report refers to as: "A party of thirsty ex-servicemen from the Ministry of Pensions Hospital, occupying an alcove above the ballroom floor". **A party of thirsty Jock ex-servicemen? It's probably their fault the Hall was closed down.**

WHAT'S IN A NAME — PART TWO

It was a Liverpool Echo misprint that was responsible for the name of one of Liverpool's most popular Mersey beat groups. The Undertakers were known as the Vegas Five until the time they appeared in the Echo's entertainment columns for their gig at the Aintree Institute as 'Undertakers'. The name Vegas Five had somehow got lost under the "Deaths". Bob Wooler told them they may as well keep the name so the group modified their act and began to use coffin shaped amplifiers and appropriate undertaker's dress. They were a very visual act who never quite made the same impact on record and they never achieved chart success. Their best effort was "If you don't come back" released in September 1964 and by then they were known as the Takers. But they were very popular in the Merseyside clubs making many appearances at the Cavern. They were voted 5th in the 1962 Mersey Beat poll, beating such acts as Gerry, Swinging Blue Jeans, Merseybeats, Dennisons, Fourmost and Rory Storm.

Brian Jones went on to play with the Gary Glitter gang and played sax on the Beatles' track "You Know My Name (Look Up The Number)" the flip side of "Let It Be". Jackie Lomax made solo records and was a backing singer to Rod Stewart. Geoff Nugent became a school caretaker. Who knows, those names may have been more familiar to us if they had remained as the Vegas Five. But then as Gerry Dorsey, Harry Webb, Ronnie Wycherley and the Quarrymen may say "What's in a name".

Undertakers and Honda's William Brown Street 1964.

THE FUN NEVER SETS ON MERSEYSIDE

"Aye, son, I don't know about Crazy Horse, more like bloody Flash Harry."

MERSEYSIDE AT PAY

Dummy pay boxes erected at the old Haymarket entrance of the Mersey Tunnel during traffic tests in 1932. Is it time the tunnel tolls disappeared altogether?

THAT'S N-ICE

It's the time of year we men hate most: the wife's birthday. What do you buy her? You've done it all, the Marks and Spencer jumper, the sexy negligée, the perfume, the jewellery, the weekend in Kirkby, two tickets for the 'derby' game (seats, of course), be honest you've simply run out of ideas.

In February 1963, butcher Alex White came up with a real cracker, he presented his wife Sheila with an ice rink, complete with a staff of 30. The rink in the former Embassy Cinema in Freshfield was named the Freshfield Winter Sports Club.

Mrs. White was better known as Sheila Dale, who in 1950 had become the first person to win both the Northern and Midland skating championships. When she won her National Skating Association gold medal in 1949 at the age of fifteen, she was one of only three other Liverpool skaters to have achieved the distinction at that time, Jeanette Altwegg and Joan Lister.

The rink was so popular, membership had reached its capacity of 6,000 before it even opened.

Liverpool Leopards 1954. Back row (left to right) George Lowry, Ron Booth, Bob Davies, George Wilde, Jeff Williamson, Larry Blackwell, Jim Parry. Front row (left to right) Eddie Birchall, Jock Duffy, Vic O'Hagan, Tony Bullock, Johnny Smith, John Gallagher.

LIVERPOOL LEOPARDS

Ice hockey was played in Liverpool before the war, but war pushed it off Merseyside's sporting calendar. So the story really begins in 1948, when a young man, Ronnie Booth, whose interest in the game had been fostered by Canadian servicemen, visited the Liverpool ice rink and decided to launch a team.

With friends Jim Parry and John Gallagher he organised a river cruise. The proceeds gave them the equipment they needed to begin.

They got a team of local boys together including Gordie Gibbons who was born in Winnipeg, Manitoba. Gibbons brought a love of the game from the wheat belt of Canada to Lancashire long before the war. He was a member of the Manchester team that was then in existence, captained the Lancashire team and played for the North of England combination side.

Then another Canadian joined them, 28-year-old Carl Sturtridge, at the time the brightest star in Liverpool's ice hockey firmament.

He was the first player to reach his half-century of goals for the club and first to reach the century.

The Leopards met Earl's Court Marlboroughs in their very first game in December 1948. They were beaten, but encouraged by a score that was close at 5-4. That season they won half of the 16 games they played, drew twice and were beaten six times.

The Leopards were disbanded in 1960, they re-formed in the seventies, but finally folded in 1982.

THE FUN NEVER SETS ON MERSEYSIDE

Stuart Hall, who brings a Byronesque or Keats like quality to his football reports, has been a regular visitor to Anfield for many years. Back in the sixties he would take his place in the press box especially early to enjoy the atmosphere generated by the Kop. So much so that before a European Cup game against Cologne in 1965 he decided to make a recording of the crowd. Stuart takes up the story.

"The wit was pouring off the Kop in torrents and I was semi conducting them. It was very emotional and when they finished I applauded them.

"I was putting my gear away, still with tears in my eyes, when this little urchin on the wall said 'Eh, mister, come 'ere'. Thinking he perhaps wanted my autograph, I went over to him. 'Yes son' I beamed. He looked me right in the eye and said 'Why don't you gerrof, you short-arsed git'."

Stuart, who has a penchant for sending up both himself and other people, had to laugh at this master stroke of debunking.

Thieves stole a half ton pillar box from outside Liverpool's Anfield ground prior to the 1987 Littlewoods Cup Final. The box is used by Liverpool F.C. staff to post tickets to successful applicants.

Winning an ice bucket seems sufficient for these fellas to be celebrating in the Vernon Arms in Dale Street.

WHAT A LARK

Deep among the wine bars, bistros, pubs and delli's of Lark Lane there is a shop, where, legend has it, you can find things that no other shop in Liverpool would even think of stocking. Where else for instance, could you find spare washers for hot water bottle stoppers or left handed tin snips.

The proprietor of this noble emporium, Norman Bros, is known to some of his regulars as the "Scouse Red Indian" for his habitual response to the many bizarre requests. "Ang on a mo," will be his reply, as he scurries off to the back to seek out right handed tin snips for someone anxious to have the set. Everything will be somewhere in the back of the shop and woe betide anyone who having asked for the near impossible doesn't return later to collect. "Yes, lad, I went scabby eyed lookin' for these and you didn't bother to show up", will be a typical greeting on your next appearance.

Clutching your left-handed tin snip you can then sample the delights of a street less than 200 yards long, one end of which is Sefton Park. Here you will find two pubs, the Masonic and the Albert, Keith's Wine Bar, Le Croissant Pattisserie, Morantos rest and gathering place (licensed) Tung Kong Chinese Restaurant, L'Allorette French cuisine, Que Pasa Mexican, as well as a take away pizza, a Greek and a Chinese take-away, the Sunshine Cafe and a soon to be opened Vegetarian and wholefood restaurant. Apart from these obvious delights there is an antique furniture restorer, the Ecumenical Christian shop, hair stylists and even the old police station is now the Lark Lane and St. Michael's Community Centre. Now, Ang on a mo, what did I do with those left-handed tin snips?

Members of the 'Kiddies Orchestra' prepare for a broadcast at BBC Liverpool in 1925. That's Uncle Toby, a 6LV resident looking on.

Teddy Dance.

THE FUN NEVER SETS ON MERSEYSIDE

AND MORE FAMOUS DOCKERS

High Noon	"I'm shooting at twelve".
Diesel	"Diesel do for the Missus".
	"Diesel do for the kid's".
Batman	Never leaves a ship without Robin.
Baldy Rabbit	Lend us a quid, I've lost me fare.
The Boss Surgeon	"Cut it out boys, cut it out".

LET'S DANCE

The summer of 1988 saw a familiar figure take to the streets of Liverpool, together with her piano. At 80 years of age Mrs. Teddy Dance not only provides entertainment to the passers by but raises thousands of pounds for local charities. Teddy played at a fringe event during International Garden Festival Year and she was so popular, she has repeated her appearances every year since then, taking up a spot in Basnett Street and playing a piano provided by nearby Rushworths. Teddy has earned lots of bread for several local hospitals and the bread link is significant as she is the real life mum of Jean Boht, Nellie Boswell in the popular TV sit-com.

EYE OF THE TIGER

He was a magnificent athlete and a great all-round, all-action fighter. He was world middleweight champion and world light heavyweight champion. He came from Nigeria, but lived, trained and fought many times in Liverpool. The theme tune from the Rocky films and Survivors No. 1 hit record could have been written with him in mind. He was Dick Tiger, one of boxing's most illustrious post war exponents. He died, tragically early in Nigeria in 1971, the same year that he retired from boxing.

Candlewick Park, San Francisco, October 23rd, 1962. Tiger leads with a left to the face of defending champion Gene Fullmer of Utah in the first round of the WBA's middleweight title fight. Tiger won a unanimous points decision.

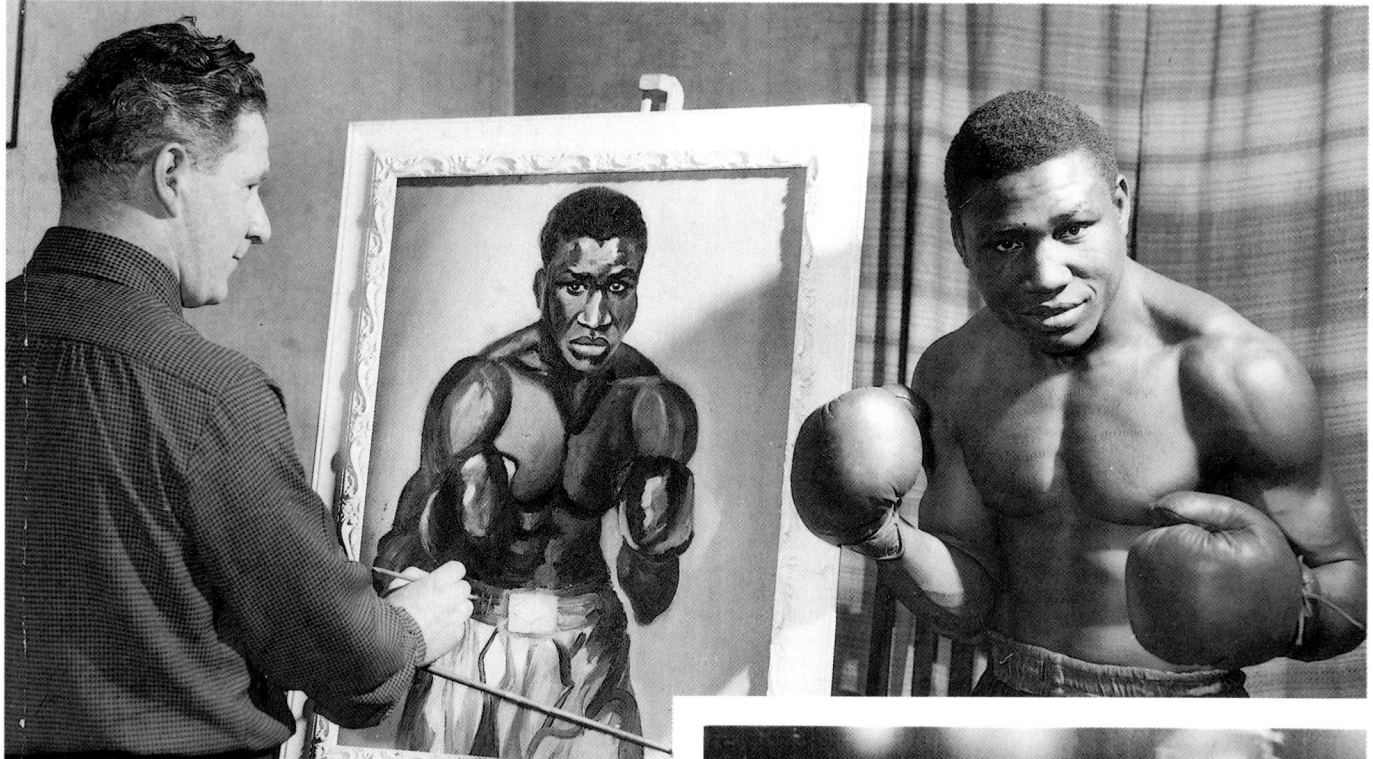

Matthew Foran of Liverpool, Tiger's trainer, completes his portrait of the champ.

Madison Square Garden, New York, December 16th, 1966, Tiger ducks to avoid a right thrown by light heavyweight champion Jose Torres. Tiger won a unanimous points decision.

THEY'LL CLEAN UP

Pictured above are Heswall Juniors hoping to clean up — together with manager and erstwhile poet, Hunt (that's him with the beard).

THE MANAGER'S SONG   *Dedicated to those who stand on the sidelines.*

He stands, collar turned up against the wind and drizzle.
The lads
look nervous, clapping and shouting,
opening the body's emergency exits for pre-match nerves.
The ref checks his watch, puts the whistle to his mouth.
A hundred similar rainy Sundays flash by him,
When he was the boy out there,
smelling the wet grass,
feeling the damp earth under his studs.
When he felt the strength of his
    mates around him.
When he felt the stomach-churning
fear of losing.
When he was one of the lads.
When he belonged.

"Look at the size of their defenders."
"How old are THEY?"
"Christ, don't our strips look tatty."
Suddenly the game's in
motion.
First touch, an easy ball, Thank God.
Running now, calling,
"Johnny, Johnny."
Not heard,
I'm out of position, get back,
chase, slide, tackle, Oh No, missed him.
He's away now,
"Well in, Pete, sorry mate."
Hand raised in admission of guilt, the slated wiped
    clean by a smile.

Run, tackle, pass, mark.
"How long till half-time, ref?"
gasping for breath.
Whistle.
One-nil down, lucky it's not three,
playing like a load of tarts.
Blood the colour of a guardsman's tunic
flows like lava from a muddy knee.
Don't remember doing that.

Change round.
Whistle.
"Let's be first, eh."
Run, chase, tackle, shoot, miss.
Pain.
Anger.
WATCH IT PAL".
"Sorry ref.".
A handshake,
respect earned,
respect given.
'Come on lads, last ten."
YEEES
"Great goal Jacko lad."
Smiles, handshakes,
relief.

A whistle blows.
The dream is gone.
But another dream's just beginning,
"Come on lads, come on . . ."

IN REVERSE ORDER — TERRY IS TOPS

In the world of bulging biceps and tree trunk like thighs Terry Phillips is a living legend. For most of us who have passed 40 and even those of us stuck on 39, it is how to cope with the next mid life crisis that occupies our thoughts not winning the Mr. Universe title. Terry Phillips, however, is not like most of us. At 18 the lad from the Scotland Road area admitted to being an eight stone weakling but from then on he started to concentrate on building up those muscles, and after spending eight years as manager of the Wooky Hollow nightclub Terry began the serious work that led him to the Mr. Universe title. At 37 he won the title, an unprecedented achievement in the body building world, as well as all the major awards, and after 40 he was Mr. Universe again. Now nearer 50 Terry runs his own health and fitness centre in Knowsley but still competes in competitions. For the diet conscious you may like to know what Terry tackles in the run up to a major championship. For breakfast 10 ounces of poached cod and a little black coffee. A tin of tuna for dinner and in the evening the same again with chicken cooked without the fat.

N.B. Terry Phillips was a four times winner of the Mr. Universe title, was Mr. World in 1986 and has won more body building titles than any other Briton.

Terry Phillips is Mr. Universe.

UP AND COMING

Photo: Alan Reekie

UP AND RUNNING

Described as Liverpool's most popular band since the Beatles
are Up and Running and many pundits believe it won't be
too long before they become nationally known. Formerly
known as 'Two's a Crowd', the band has sold out Liverpool's
Royal Court and Empire Theatre's and their singles 'Sorry'
and 'Johnny and Marie' have both topped the local best
sellers.

NOT ALL PLAY

In 1957 Liverpool Institute School won nine Mathematics
scholarships to Cambridge — a British record.

THE FUN NEVER SETS ON MERSEYSIDE

Doreen from Knotty Ash was telling her friend how
she'd 'inhaled a taxi'.

Her friend was laughing her head off.

"You are funny Doreen," she said, "you're always
coming out with those Molatov's".

It was a bitterly cold day in the Goodison stand and
at half time big George shouted to his friend Charlie
sitting at the end of the row.

"Hey, Charlie, you're nearest, go and get the
drinks".

After checking the order with the rest of the group
George shouted "Six oxo's Charl".

Charlie a little less than enthusiastically got up only
to return a few minutes later.

"How many sugars did yis want?"

*Mathew Street, Liverpool, in its time the location of the Cavern, Erics, the
Liverpool School of Language. Music Dream and Pun, Carl Jungs bust,
O'Halligans parlour, the Grapes Eat ya Heart Out bistro, Arthur Dooley's Beatles
tribute, the Armadilla Tea Rooms, the Left Bank Bistro, Cavern Walks — and
Liverpool sculptur Charlie Alexander apparently dressed as a Tarzan Kissogram,
leaps from one of the imposing warehouses into . . . . . .*

A bowl of custard! — Celebrating at the Carl Jung festival in 1978 — a sponsored custard plunge.

Liverpool's karate superstar Frank Brennan, a member of the world famous Liverpool Red Triangle Club.

Ann Hughes, a world judo champion from Crosby.

THE FUN NEVER SETS ON MERSEYSIDE

The passenger asked the Scouse deck hand on the Llandudno boat, "Where is Deganwy?" He replied, "At de other end of de ship".

The Liverpool priest was a keen golfer but he frowned upon his parishioners playing on a Sunday. One Saturday he finished his round in disastrous fashion, doing a nine on the par 5 eighteenth hole. He couldn't get to sleep that night thinking about his awful form and at 3 am on Sunday morning he sneaked back to the course to attempt the hole again. Peter and Paul spotted him and gave The Boss a shout straight away. "I'll fix him". said God.

The Priest teed off and the ball soared 300 yards down the fairway, straight as a die. He'd never hit one so far. He hit his second shot with a No. 3 iron and as the dawn broke he watched in amazement as the ball struck the green and on the second bounce went into the hole.

"I thought you were going to punish him?" said Peter.

"I have", replied God, "who's he going to tell and even if he does who is going to believe him?"

A young man went into Liverpool to see the celebrations of a city store's Centenary. Miss Liverpool was due to arrive in a stagecoach. He waited outside the entrance where a small queue had formed when a woman came up and asked him if he was waiting for the bus. Politely he replied, "No the stagecoach". "Don't be so bloody funny," said the woman.

TO ALL THE SIX ROUND HEROES

In February 1987 the death sentence was passed on one of Britain's greatest sporting venues. The Liverpool Stadium was to be demolished.

A structural survey had revealed the building to be unsafe, and the cost of rebuilding was prohibitive.

The story of the Stadium, opened in 1932 as Britain's only purpose-built boxing arena, to replace the old Pudsey Street Stadium, has been well documented, especially in the First Whitbread Book of Scouseology. The Stadium was the working man's theatre in Liverpool, and it is through the lives of the local journeymen fighters, that the true importance of the Stadium can be seen. Many old boxing fans, and old boxers, remember the fights between long forgotten battlers, rather than the big occasions.

One such fighter was Paddy Nolan, and on the closure of the Stadium his brother Lol, wrote eloquently about the life of a 'six round hero.'

"My brother Paddy was a boxer. He was unfortunate to have a promising career cut short by the outbreak of war. He turned pro and had over 100 bouts while still working at his full-time job as a sheet metalworker on the Dock Road.

Regularly working a 70 hour week, which kept him as fit as a fiddle, he boxed whenever and wherever the opportunity occurred.

My fondest memory was when they held Sunday afternoon shows. One week the late Johnny Best booked him for an eight rounder against a tough Glaswegian, Jock Moore.

On the Friday before the fight he was roped in to work all day Saturday and Sunday on an urgent job, and he contacted Mr. Best to cry off.

He was told it was too late to find a substitute and that he would have to fight. Finally he agreed to box, provided his fight went on first, rather than immediately before the top of the bill.

The Stadium, November 1955, Liverpool's Billy Ellaway and 'Kit' Pompey in an action moment. Ellaway won on points.

Paddy's dinner break was from noon to 1.00 pm, and the show started at 1.00 pm. He went to work that morning with his boxing gear on underneath a boiler suit, borrowed a workmate's bike, and cycled to the Stadium. Putting up one of the most hectic performances of his life he knocked out the Scot in the 5th with a right uppercut. He had the gloves off almost before the referee had finished counting, and left the ring. He got back to work by 1.30, and considered himself lucky to only lose an hour's pay.

Despite being a great favourite at the Stadium he never did get a title fight, and later joined the fairground boxing booths, where he found he could earn more money.

He had something like 700 booths fights over the years, and on one particular Saturday in Sefton Park he had 17 fights and won every one by a knockout."

Before the Stadium was demolished the ring was raffled among local boxing clubs, giving youngsters the chance to step onto the famous canvas.

With the passing of the Stadium another slice of city's heritage has fallen beneath the wrecker's ball.

As Alan Rudkin said:

"It is the Liverpool kids I feel sorry for.

"When I was a youngster you always had the dream of boxing at the Stadium, and for many of us it became a reality.

"I first boxed there at the age of 13 in Schoolboy championships, and even to this day I can remember travelling there on the Overhead Railway from the Dingle where I lived. But kids now won't have this opportunity.

"It has always been special for me, and the big thing is that it was built just as a boxing arena.

"I remember Lennox Beccles coming over here in 1967 to box Johnny Cooke for the Empire title. One of the Beccles team stood with me in the tunnel where the boxers make their entrance, and after surveying the scene he told me he had been to some great fight centres around the world, but the Stadium beat them all. There was nothing like it anywhere."

. . . .

Signing the visitors' book at Birkenhead Town Hall is Pat McAteer, a member of one of Britain's most famous boxing families. He was attending a reception in his honour to mark his British title win in 1955. That's Wally Thom and Alderman T. Anderson and Mrs. Anderson. McAteer went to live in the States after his retirement where he is a successful businessman.

One of Liverpool's most popular boxers, former British Welterweight champion Johnny Cooke pictured attending a sportsman's dinner in Liverpool with Henry Cooper in 1972. Dare we suggest he looks just a little like Mrs. Butler's eldest son . . . . . Johnny not Henry.

A celebrity boxing line-up at the Stadium in 1957. Standing (left to right) Albert Demmy, Jimmy Stewart, Billy Gannon, Nat Williams, Tony Butcher, J. E. Balshaw, Douglas Collister, Martin Hansen, Johnny Best, Jack Hanlon, Reg Gregory. Front (left to right) Ron Jones, Gus Foran, Jimmy Brown, Hogan Bassey, Wally Thom, Norman James.

The 'Phil gives a children's concert at the Stadium in 1951.

Yesterday's hero . . . And a hall filled with memories.

READER'S RESPONSE

The place — somewhere in Merseyside.
The people — A typical Merseyside couple.
The year — unknown.
All you have to do is to supply an appropriate Scouse caption and send it off to:

WHITBREAD BOOK OF SCOUSEOLOGY
CAPTION COMPETITION
SCOUSE PROMOTIONS LTD.
8 MATHEW STREET, LIVERPOOL L2 6RE

The best decided by the judges will receive a prize during 1989.

The authors and publishers wish to thank all the photographers represented in this book for so brilliantly capturing the images of Merseyside, and wish to thank them for permission to use their work.
Our thanks also to those we were unable to trace or contact.

THE SCOUSEOLOGY PICTURE QUIZ ANSWERS?

PQ1   The hydraulic power station at Canada Dock built in 1857.
PQ2   Harvey Smith.
PQ3   It's Margaret Lockwood.
PQ4   Ian and the Zodiacs flying to appear in the U.S.A. in 1965. They were originally refused work permits.
PQ5   Joe Baker signing for Arsenal in 1962. That's Torino's representative Gigi Peronace on the left.
PQ6   Roadrunners.
PQ7   Liverpool lost 1-0.
PQ8   Frankie Vaughan.
PQ9   The Merseyside Barbershop Harmony Club.
PQ10   The floral clock in Woolton Wood.
PQ11   Muriel Cronshaw of course.
PQ12   Bootle women A.R.P. about to visit every home in the district on a gas mask fitting demonstration in September 1938. They had three different sizes of gas masks and a bottle of disinfectant each.
PQ13   1954.
PQ14   Inside St. George's Hall organ.
PQ15   Newsham Park.
PQ16   1958.
PQ17   The first Chinese newspaper in Britain Hua Chow Pao (Chinese Weekly News) comes off the press.
PQ18   Wavertree.
PQ19   Gerry Marsden.
PQ20   St. Mary's Highfield Street.
N.B.   If you got the newspaper name correct in question 17 (in Chinese of course) award yourself a bonus mark of ten.

ANSWERS

Mersey Film Teasers (page 57).
1. Basil Rathbone — Anna Karenina.
2. Picton Road, College Road, Boaler Street, Mill Street Dingle.
3. RSM Brittain (loudest voice in the British Army) uncle of cyclist Stan.
4. John Gregson.
5. Charles Chrichton.

Mersey Pop Teasers (page 93).
1. O.M.D. Dindisc.
2. China Crisis.
3. Michael Holliday.
4. Burt Bacharach/Hilliard.
5. The Merseybeats.
6. Del Shannon 'From Me To You', in June 1963.
7. Lee Curtis.
8. 'Love Is Like A Violin'.
9. Wah.
10. Ramon Remedios.

QUIZ & TEASER ANSWERS

The Third Man (page 93) is Jimmy Tarbuck.

Our intrepid journalists (page 22) Mr. Key and Mr. Trollope are attending the press conference in March 1981 of Ken Campbell's satire "War with the Newts" which was performed at the Everyman. The press conference was held in the Adelphi swimming pool.

. . . .

This book is dedicated to the people of Merseyside past, present and future, who 'put on a show'

to George Glover one of Merseyside's unsung heroes.

It's a Sunday afternoon in late autumn and a weak sun tries hard to penetrate through the trees in Woolton Woods. Sometimes, but not often, there just isn't anyone to play with . . .